Learning to
Prosper

LEARNING TO PROSPER

FINANCIAL SUCCESS AFTER YOUR MISSION

DUSTIN ROBISON

CFI
Springville, Utah

ISBN 13: 978-1-59955-232-3

Published by CFI, an imprint of Cedar Fort, Inc., 2373 W. 700 S., Springville, UT 84663
Distributed by Cedar Fort, Inc., www.cedarfort.com

LIBRARY OF CONGRESS CATALOGING-IN-PUBLICATION DATA
Robison, Dustin.
Learning to prosper / Dustin Robison.
p. cm.
ISBN 978-1-59955-232-3
1. Church of Jesus Christ of Latter-day Saints--Missions. 2. Mormon Church--Missions. 3. Mormon missionaries. 4. Finance, Personal--Religious aspects--Church of Jesus Christ of Latter-day Saints. 5. Finance, Personal--Religious aspects--Mormon Church. I. Title.

BX8661.R63 2009
266'.93--dc22

2008041851

Cover design by Angela D. Olsen
Cover design © 2009 by Lyle Mortimer
Edited and typeset by Melissa J. Caldwell

Printed in the United States of America

10 9 8 7 6 5 4 3 2 1

Printed on acid-free paper

Contents

1

UNDERSTANDING WEALTH: Money Is a Necessity

So you've served your mission, and now it's time to get married, have kids, and earn a living as you continue to establish the kingdom. This is a very exciting time in your life and, at the same time, very intimidating (maybe a little socially awkward without the name tag and companion). It's time to find an eternal companion and decide on an enjoyable profession that will support you and your family for the remainder of your mortal journey.

These tasks will require some money. You could do a few things—perhaps dating—without spending much, but you will definitely be needing cash at this stage in your life. A phone, gas, food, housing, insurance, entertainment, education, transportation and all kinds of other things you'll be doing will cost money. It's time to learn how to obtain that shiny penny so that life can go on.

Live On!

May I say one very important thing about this point in your life before continuing? You might be thinking this, and I'm sure you've heard it stated many times . . . "the mission was the greatest two years of my life." I don't apologize to anybody when I say that it shouldn't be! Your mission is a solid, testimony-building experience that you will continue to build on for the rest of your life. If you apply the principles and teachings that you learned as a missionary, I promise you that life will only get better with each passing year.

This is coming from a guy who loved his mission and never once has considered it as two years of difficult work or miserable sacrifice. I had a blast during my mission and wouldn't change anything about it. Nevertheless, I feel that I've grown and have been blessed beyond measure since returning. I know that you can continue to have the best years of your life after your mission. Consider making every year the best year as you strive to make every day the best day of your life!

Money ≠ Wickedness, Money ≠ Righteousness

An important concept about money that you need to understand up front is that money is not evil, and moreover, money *is not righteousness*! I don't wish to argue the doctrine behind the popular belief that money is evil. You have to earn money in this life, and there is absolutely nothing wrong with wanting to earn plenty of it. If money becomes your god and your obsession, obviously, that is evil. If, out of greed, you don't pay your tithing, your fast offerings, or help the needy, money can be evil.

Unfortunately, many have faded into perdition because of an obsession with riches. There aren't near as many rich people in this world as there are average income or poor people—am I right? With such a high percentage of the few rich people falling away, is there any wonder that so many preach against it? I know several individuals that will not hesitate to tell you that wanting to be wealthy is evil. Seeking eternal riches should certainly be objective number one, and as long as you can maintain that proper perspective, you're safe. Those alarmed and feeling an obligation to warn you of your "evil" desires to obtain wealth have no right to make you feel guilty, for a rich man can be just as righteous as a beggar (and vice versa).

I, at times, feel like it's comparable to the pretty-girl syndrome (applicable to males as well): a beautiful woman walks into a room full of other women, and the natural tendency is for the perhaps jealous onlookers to start developing negative thoughts and commentaries about the new presence. They pick her apart and analyze any weakness they can find. Don't believe me? Watch one episode of the hit TV show called *The Bachelor*. Being what others want to but are unable to be for one reason or another is like painting a target for negative attention. The masses that would love to be rich can easily shrug it off as a righteous motivation not to be. There are people who truly have no desire whatsoever to have an abundance of wealth, but I'd be willing to bet that the less fortunate who criticize those that successfully seek after prosperity would switch places in a heartbeat, if they could.

Some honestly believe that being rich is morally wrong, and I don't wish to criticize their personal beliefs, but I sincerely hope that they don't convert anybody into financial inactivity. Siddhartha Gautama, more commonly known as Buddha, popularized the teaching of procuring a happy medium by avoiding extremes. He was born into rich nobility and forsook everything to find more meaning in life. Other Greek philosophers such as Socrates spread similar teachings of mediocrity as a means of obtaining true happiness, and these ideas have spread throughout the world for centuries.

I can't really blame those who preach against personal wealth, but I believe that a man can be rich without risking his eternal salvation. We'll turn out all right as long as we can avoid becoming as the young rich man who asked Jesus how he could gain eternal life and walked away sadly, because "he had many possessions" that he couldn't give up. We must not obsess over riches. Keep in mind the willing heart of Lehi, who left all of his material possessions, which were many, because God had other plans for him.

God Wants You to Be Prosperous

Doctrine and Covenants 38:39: "And if ye seek the riches which it is the will of the Father to give unto you, ye shall be the richest of all people, for ye shall have the riches of eternity; and it must needs be that the riches of the earth are mine to give; but beware of pride, lest ye become as the Nephites of old."

According to this scripture, Heavenly Father wants us to obtain riches—both temporal and spiritual. We are warned to avoid becoming as the Nephites of old, who quickly forgot about God as they grew rich. You can read about this in chapter 13 of Helaman. Read verses 18–23 especially to get a better understanding of the pride cycle.

Please, do not ever mistake wealth for righteousness either. I believe there are many more members of the LDS faith that fall into this category than into the former. I had several bishoprics as I moved from one ward to another at BYU. Without fail, almost every compliment I heard about a leader's spirituality was tied directly to his money. "Our bishop is so great . . . you gotta see his house. He's loaded!" As a matter of fact, I've heard at least three more similar comments since I began writing this book just a few months ago.

I've even found evidence that illustrates this pitfall of "righteousness by riches" as I've spoken with individuals that have been called to certain leadership positions. I can honestly say that if there is one calling I aspire to, it would be that of a mission president. I appreciate the occasions I have here to associate with those that have been called as mission presidents, and I enjoy asking them what things I might do in life to one day have such an opportunity myself. I recall asking one individual whose response confused me a little. His exact words: "Dustin, you need to subdue the earth. Make as much money as you can in a righteous way, and you will be blessed." Needless to say I was taken back by his answer and couldn't comprehend his logic. Maybe I misunderstood his point, but the message I got was that I needed to be rich if I had any hopes of being called to serve in such a capacity.

Contrary to popular belief, Church leaders do not need to be rich to be called. My mission president was a less-than-rich high school principal from Argentina who never served a mission (he converted after he married), was never a bishop, and never had any other calling of considerable leadership. God made it very clear that he would use the weak and simple men of his Church to spread his gospel (D&C 1:23).

Americans Are Wealthier Than They Know

Last, whether you know it or not, you already enjoy luxuries beyond the imagination of most of the world's population. Even if you seem poor according to American standards, you are not! I've found several different quotes from no definite source about a person with clothes on her back, food in the fridge, and a roof over her head being richer than 75 percent of the world. If you've bought this book, you're probably closer to the top fifth percentile. The freedoms and privileges you are blessed with as a member of the Church and a citizen of the United States of America can easily be taken for granted.

People die every day while attempting to get into this country of prosperity and equality . . . over five hundred people gave their lives between the U.S. and Mexico border in the year 2005.[1] Why? They live in countries with unpaved roads and huts where politics and police are corrupt beyond comprehension; air conditioners are unheard of along with washing machines, refrigerators, hot water heaters, computers, iPods, TVs, and too many other things to enumerate. Education and employment are extremely difficult to come by, and it is literally impossible to ever obtain a consistent and sufficient income. I recently heard a news report about countries in India and Africa where the daily wage is equivalent to a meager 50 cents! Here, you almost have to try to be poor in order to truly experience poverty. Whether you live in a single-wide trailer out in the desert or a mansion in Beverly Hills, you can be grateful that you're not in a foreign country where it can be much worse.

Money Is More Than a Job

More than likely, you know absolutely nothing about money . . . except for the whole job concept. At least, I didn't have a very good understanding about money when I returned home from Peru. I was ready to go to college, because that's what the world expects. I would major in something I found interesting while knocking out my prerequisites for dental school. Dentists earn a great income and have very convenient schedules! That's all I knew, and it's all I cared to know.

I often spent time hanging out with a couple of mission companions that loved to talk about their goals of earning money—and lots of it. Every time we got together there was some new elaborate scheme that was sure to be profitable. I thought it was pure gibberish and not once did I consider joining in on their conversations, because I had never even imagined creating my own wealth.

Parents, teachers, and leaders had guided me down the path of making good grades and preparing to enter the world of jobs after my mission. Funny how that's the focus. "Perform well at school so you can get a job; you'll never get a real job unless you go to college; you'll never get into college unless you work hard now." They say it a million different ways, and for the most part, it's true. It's a proven system wherein security and safety can be found . . . but a little limiting if you ask me.

Working for Yourself Might Be More Rewarding

What they don't tell you is that there are alternatives to jobs. Instead of being an employee, you can become an employer! Now that's food for thought, isn't it? What's even more bizarre for me is that my dad was an entrepreneur—a man who ran several of his own businesses and is very successful at what he does—but rarely did he train me on the concept of creating an income for myself. I might have been too thick-headed for anything he was trying to teach me to sink in. He did buy a parking lot paint striping machine at one point and helped me get some bidding forms together to solicit jobs from local businesses, but at the age of thirteen, I was way too afraid to ever ask any adult managers to hire me.

Money Principles Should Be Learned at a Young Age

I'm not an anti-job advocate, but I feel like we should be instructed at least somewhat concerning money as we go through junior high and high school. Not one class offered in my high school had anything to do with money or wealth. We did play a stock market game once in a history class as we entered the era of the Great Depression. I got really rich with fake money and then lost everything! The question I always ask myself is why in the world would something so important never even be mentioned in thirteen years of education? You know, my *college* curriculum *also* failed to teach me anything specific about wealth. That's crazy!

My point is that everything concerning money was about getting a job to earn money. There are several great jobs in the world that will bring you happiness and allow you to live a comfortable life of wealth. If you choose to be traditional and earn your wages as an employee who is making his boss rich, I wish you all the happiness that a person can find, but I hope that by reading this book you will realize that there are other options.

Utah, home of the majority of the Church's returned missionaries, produces more entrepreneurs than most other places in the world. I believe that has a lot to do with the principles and work ethics learned on a mission. Even if you find a great paying job, you can still do things on the side that might be more enjoyable and more profitable for you. You could possibly find a way to retire much earlier than you ever would have otherwise.

Don't Be Blinded by Traditional J-O-Bs

A quick example: I taught Spanish part-time at the MTC for three years and loved it. This was a very high-paying student job and extremely sought after at BYU. Having this job meant I had to be at work on time every day and attend several weekly meetings/trainings (about twenty-four hours per week). This "high-paying job" was good enough to get me through several years of school, pay for some dates, feed me, and allow me to squeak by from month to month. Did it cover everything? Nope.

Had my job not been so fun and spiritually uplifting, I definitely wouldn't have been there very long. I actually always felt like it was more of a scholarship than a job . . . being with the missionaries really wasn't work. It didn't take me much time, though, to figure out that there were other ways to make the money I needed. While teaching, I started experimenting with entrepreneurial ventures and opened a business that I still profit from to this day.

Recently, I woke up after a full night of rest, came to my store a little late (I would probably fire myself if I could), did some company work, and spent time writing this book. I had already earned more money that day than I did during a whole month of teaching Spanish . . . and there was nothing extraordinary about business that day. That's not even counting the income accumulated from my side investments. Just a couple days ago, I made more money in four hours of working for myself than I would in two whole months working as a Spanish teacher. It would've taken me over two hundred hours of my job to equal my earnings accumulated in just four hours as my own boss!

Smart Work

Learn how to work smart and you won't have to work hard . . . although working hard is a very good thing to do. Better put—you can work hard and see much greater results in a shorter amount of time! What I do is nothing revolutionary. I buy things and I resell them for a profit. I'm what you might call a "dealer." Doing "deals" is one of a few basic ways to make a buck . . . or a million! You don't have to be incredibly smart or a great salesman to make it happen.

Graduate with No Debt

In this book I will explain how systems can be put into place that earn you money while you do anything you want (like writing books). The goal you should have for yourself now is to graduate from college with *no debt*, own some *solid investments*, and have *money in the bank*.

Exercise Agency to Control Your Destiny

You might get rich and you might not. To a large degree, man is responsible for his own fate, but there is only so much that you *can* control. I believe that many people are very capable of building currency into a bank account, but sometimes Heavenly Father doesn't want them to. I can't say why he wouldn't want some individuals not to have very much money, but there is wisdom in all things that he does.

Money could be and often is the spiritual downfall of a good person. With money comes opportunity, and many people use monetary opportunity to do spiritually destructive things. With money comes pride and a sense of independence. If you're an RM, I need not remind you about the pride cycle and how it works.

While God has ultimate control over what happens around us, there is still the governing principle of agency. If you choose to obtain riches and work for them the right way, I don't see why he would stop you indefinitely. He might put up protective obstacles if having money will harm your eternal salvation, but if it's your choice and determination, he will let the earth and the laws that govern it run their course.

At the same time, there are many people that God has willed to be financially wealthy. I know several people that seem to have money thrown at them for no other reason than being in the right place at the right time . . . all the time! You will meet people like this as well, and it's hard not to be envious. My only words of wisdom on this particular point—don't covet your neighbor's ass (see Exodus 20:17).

Define Wealth

Would you say a man who has an enjoyable occupation that he's very good at, a close family that he spends several hours with daily, a small home, $20,000 in savings, a working mini-van, two weeks of vacation every year, several friends, a fishing pole, his one year of food storage, and even a dog named Skip is wealthy? What does wealth mean? Being wealthy doesn't necessarily mean that you have money pouring down from heaven. I know you don't need money to be happy. That doesn't mean, however, that poverty isn't miserable.

Where I served my mission was one of the poorest countries in the world, but I recognized almost instantly that the people in general were very happy and cheerful. However, most of the Peruvian men I met woke up at some time around 5:00 AM to go work and would return at 10:00 or 11:00 PM only to earn a meager $3.00 or $4.00/day (that's *if* they had a job). With an income too small to even feed your family, could you be happy? I doubt I would find myself bursting with joy.

Dream Big

Some people want a life of distinguished wealth and financial prosperity, but most are content with mediocrity. Do you fall into one of these categories, or do you find yourself somewhere in between? I hope for your sake and your family's that you wish to build an empire. You should want the best for yourself, your loved ones, and any fellow man that you might be able to assist. Settling for anything less than what you are capable of is cheating yourself of growth, wisdom, experience, knowledge, dominion, and fulfillment that you are completely entitled to. Don't ever let anyone make you feel guilty for aspiring to something more than an average life.

In this book, you will be enlightened by several financial principles that can lead you to a life of prosperity. If you want to graduate college completely debt free and have the freedom and confidence to pursue your extraordinary ambitions, this book can help guide the way. I know you have the motivation, and I know you have the ability, so *make sure* you have the willingness to actually do the exercises at the end of the chapters hereafter. The experience and knowledge you are about to obtain will change your life and your family's for the better.

Note

1. Wikipedia, "Migrant Deaths along the Mexico–United States Border," http://en.wikipedia.org/wiki/Immigrant_deaths_along_the_U.S.-Mexico_border.

2

Audacity to Become

Hernando Cortez left Spain in 1519 with six hundred men, fewer than twenty horses, and ambitions to colonize Mexico. After suppressing the town of Tabasco, he and his troops went north to settle a better sea port now called Vera Cruz. Hernando Cortez was in Mexico to conquer and nothing would stop him . . . his motto was "conquer or die" (*conquistador* literally means "conqueror").

To prevent any thought of retreat, Cortez had his whole fleet of ships burned to a crisp. This was an audacious move that proved very fortunate for his plans as he soon discovered the Aztec empire. He moved his troops inland and fooled the Aztec people into believing that he was Quetzalcoatl, the great white God that had visited long before and promised to one day return (interesting history for a Latter-day Saint).

Cortez, a man who was victorious in a battle where his troops were *outnumbered 300 to 1,* miraculously overthrew the Aztec kingdom and achieved what he set out to accomplish. I can think of no better example of audacity, bravery, and courage than the colonization of Mexico by the renowned conquistador Hernando Cortez. Although I don't condone war or killing for land, it impresses me that he burned every option of failure and overcame staggering odds to find success.

Conquer Your World

How many missionaries conquer a whole new world during their two years of service? Pretty much every single one. Do you recall the courage it took to leave everything you knew and loved in life to go somewhere you had never been before, perhaps speaking a language you didn't know, and with little more than your scriptures, some white shirts, and a handful of ties? There are few feats that measure up to such an experience. It requires courage and faith to make the decision to serve a full-time mission and then follow through with it.

You learned an immeasurable number of techniques, methodologies, doctrines, and language skills in a miraculous time frame. You developed lasting relationships constantly from one area to another and had no choice but to start fresh every time you were transferred. To pack up your belongings every two to six months and move to a completely new area where you did not know one single person requires a special personality. It requires the personality of a creative, adaptive, dynamic go-getter. That is why you have what it takes to be successful in this life.

You Are an Elite Individual

Imagine the billions of spirit children that have come to this earth, that are here right now, and that are yet to come. Of the mind-boggling number of Heavenly Father's children, you are one of the few blessed with the opportunity to have the truth about God's plan made known to you. Tremendous responsibilities have been placed on your shoulders and a trust that only the Lord's elect are privileged to receive. This is because you are special, unique, and bold enough to do something with the gifts that you are given. An individual that can accomplish so much on a spiritual level surely has been endowed with the capability of achieving great and marvelous things on a temporal level. The main ingredient is a *belief in yourself* if you wish to do extraordinary things.

Learn to be Extraordinary

Daring to do what your high school buddies or college classmates do not is a distinguishing character trait that you must develop if you do not already possess it. We've already talked about the traditional philosophies of finance and job security. Most people will not veer from the path that has been trodden by our parents and grandparents. Most people will play things safe and never even consider thinking outside the box. Did you know that most people will live their entire lives drowning in bad debt? Most people will retire at sixty-five after working forty- or fifty-hour weeks with little to no control over their lives, and they will continue to live paycheck to paycheck until the day they pass away.

The time to be bold is now! I'm sorry to inform you that there is no idiot-proof system that I'm aware of to guarantee you success in this life.

You might find yourself in bankruptcy or foreclosure for reasons that are impossible to anticipate. You could be on top of the world one day, and the next, everything could blow up in your face. Many people are forced to endure an unavoidable turn of events that leads them into hard times. You know exactly what hard times are good for . . . making you stronger!

Why You Can Beat the Odds

If you want to play it safe in life, at least be willing to take some risks while you're still young. If your financial situation heads south this early in the game, you'll have plenty of time to make up for it. Those who wait until they're thirty-five or forty to start risking a little money, time, and energy in hopes of earning more than their current job pays are those who might never recover from a failed attempt.

Statistically, you are going against the odds when you try to be original and create streams of income that are different or unknown. Let me be the one to point out that these business statistics are drastically skewed. It is widely believed that 80 percent of all businesses fail within the first five years of operation. These numbers include businesses that were only designed to operate on a niche market for a few years. Not all business ideas will last forever, and several ventures could be very profitable in a one to five year period. These misleading numbers also include those who are anxious enough to go waste their money on a business license for some spontaneous idea that wasn't thought out very well and was never executed.

I overheard one lady closing out her business license at the city hall say that she never even did anything to get her business going. I believe the majority of those failures that the statistics show can be attributed to individuals who did the exact same thing—they had an idea, created a name for it, bought a license, went home, and just waited for the money to come, thinking that they were done with the hard part, Success demands a lot more than a business license. You have to be brave enough to get out there and make things happen.

Conquer Your Fears

Allow me to use myself as a bad example on this point. As I write this book, I have a business idea in my back pocket that requires little start-up costs and that I am certain will gross millions of dollars in revenue each year. I have ideas on a weekly, if not daily, basis, but this one is the epitome of every business idea I've ever conceived. I have already laid the footwork for this idea by coming up with a business plan, building a website for it, preparing some necessary publications, and naming it. I haven't started it yet for a few reasons, but I'm aware that the number one reason I'm not making this happen is *fear.*

I have some goals I want to accomplish before being distracted by another business venture, but I admit without hesitation that I am scared to death to start something new that may fail. This is a common sentiment when it comes to the life of an entrepreneur. If you are smart, you will recognize that fear is to be expected and that it must not be allowed to dominate your decisions.

It is scary when you realize that you cannot pay for your mortgage payment if your business doesn't perform. It's a little frightening to think that you will have to invest so much time, emotion, energy, and capital into something that might not pan out. With a spouse depending on you to perform financially and bring home the bread, fear can take over.

I spoke with a friend recently who has invested over $200,000 dollars in a business franchise that will not have positive cash flow for almost an entire year. Although he's optimistic, I could hear his worries in the tone of his voice. That's why so many people opt for the job. They go to the guy who took the risk, who set up a successful system for generating income, and who is making millions. They ask if they can help earn his money for him in return for a small cut—also known as a salary or a wage.

Develop the Go-Getter Attitude

I wish I knew how to instill this attitude into your soul, but I don't have the words to express it. You must take risks! You must take chances! You must be bold! You must believe in yourself! You must not bow down to fear! Reject this advice and you welcome with open arms a mediocre life of boredom and dissatisfaction. Don't get me wrong . . . fear is good to have and prevents us from committing stupid mistakes, but when it comes to financial freedom, we must not be afraid to risk a little. Considering that everything about life involves risk, I sincerely hope that you properly measure and manage the risk factor pertaining to money.

The most common obstacle for an average person is that he has already convinced himself that *he can't.* I've seen it countless times . . . you can explain to somebody a guaranteed method of making a quick profit, and he almost always tunes out about halfway through the conversation.

Why? He's always told himself that he can't do that—that making money requires money and since he doesn't have any, there's no point in trying.

I've explained as logically as I know how to on several occasions, that a person can earn good money by investing in a home, and pay no more than he pays with rent, which is nothing but throwing money away. I explain this to qualified home buyers, but they are inevitably convinced that they can't buy a house. I'm a licensed loan officer and know what it takes to qualify for a home loan, but I always find people who just won't believe me when I tell them they could and should purchase a home. They've never thought about it, but the concept of owning a home seems like a dream, so they stop listening and can't be convinced that it's a possibility. Realize today that you have to knock down this ridiculous obstacle of self-pity. You can make anything happen if you truly want to. Conquer your fears and you can "conquistar" the world.

Exercise:

Do things you are normally afraid to do! Ask out that beautiful girl you've had your eye on for the last couple of months. Go rappelling down a mountain if you're afraid of heights. Try new foods. Talk to people in public places when you don't have to. Travel outside of your comfort zone frequently, and it could change your life. It's a great habit to consistently push yourself to do good things that you aren't normally comfortable with doing.

In a monetary sense, make an investment that involves some risk. Buy some stocks and see what happens (do your research and make sure you buy the right stocks of course). Learn what real estate options and assignments are and go exercise one (requires little or no money). Find a promising business idea, and start your own company. We will expound on how to do these things in later chapters. Within the next six months, choose one or more of these options and make it happen. Overcome your inhibitions and be audacious.

3

Use Missionary Skills in Whatever You Do

Think back to that first day in the mission field. You were so glad to get out of the confinements of the MTC. Whether you spent three weeks, nine weeks, or twelve weeks in the labyrinth of brown brick walls, the last seven to ten days were insanely long! You knew it all and thought that you had gleaned everything out of the MTC experience that a missionary could . . . then, reality sank in as you began your first day of proselyting in the field. Prayers for divine help intensified, and a feeling of complete dependence on your companion and the Lord took over. You had no idea where you were or how to work effectively, and perhaps you couldn't understand a single word that the people around you were speaking. The reality of not knowing diddly squat hit you pretty hard.

A humbling experience like a mission called for an incredible amount of information, skills, and techniques to be learned. I'm still amazed at everything I was able to accomplish during two short years and know that it was only through Heavenly Father's hand that I was sustained. My mission president, Belisario Benites, taught that it would take forty years for a normal member to learn and grow as much as a missionary does in two. I'm sure you'll agree. And we all know that the sisters only need eighteen months to accomplish what an elder does in twenty-four. You've acquired some of the most essential work habits and time management skills that make success a possibility. Now, it's time to apply everything you learned as a missionary to your studies, career, church callings, and family life.

Those who complete a full-time mission and hit the ground running upon returning home are sure to see better results than those who forget all about it. What I mean is that some keep right on living like they did as a missionary . . . except for the whole opposite sex situation. They keep a schedule, define their goals, work, study, pray and the list goes on. Others arrive home with an attitude that they've put in their time and are now done! They sleep all day, slack off in their Church activities, watch hours of TV, and do all kinds of things that lead them to being desensitized to the things of the Spirit. A life of productivity suddenly turns into a life of apathetic passiveness—comfortable inactivity. Be the person with enough zeal to keep up the pace!

A missionary develops quite an extensive list of attributes in the field, which should be applied to mission afterlife. Enumerating a few and discussing how they apply might be helpful. You learned social skills (relationship building), communication (with companion, leaders, investigators, and family), cleanliness and order, presentation, study habits, leadership skills, teaching skills, team work, pragmatic planning, punctuality, persuasion, record keeping, responsibility, discipline, happiness, balancing schedules, and overcoming rejection, to name a few. We won't go into details about all of these, but I suggest writing them down along with other attributes that you acquired and analyzing them so that you can better apply them to your present circumstances.

One of my very first memories of arriving to the field is the time my companion and I took to discuss our goals and the planning session that followed. This principle of pragmatic planning is simply the first and foremost duty for productive action. For this reason, the entire next chapter is dedicated to the exploration of visionary planning and getting up out of bed to make it happen. In this chapter, we will explore some of the other essentials you adopted as a missionary and that you will need throughout life.

Social Skills

Developing social skills was among the most valuable lessons that you learned in the field. If you couldn't talk to people very well or develop a sense of friendship within seconds of meeting them, the only way you got to teach people was if your companion could! Being transferred every six weeks to eight months meant leaving everything and everybody you knew behind and starting fresh in a brand new area. New companions, new leaders, new members, and new investigators were thrust upon you (and every single one expected you to be as cool as the missionary you were replacing). You met total strangers thousands of times during your days as a missionary. It was absolutely vital to be socially dynamic. The same relationship skills are fundamental in the world of monetary gain. At the base of nearly every business transaction is a relationship!

Some missionaries are naturally social butterflies but most need to develop and fine-tune their people skills. My patriarchal blessing tells me that I will develop socially throughout life, and I've seen that come to pass. I'm still a long ways away from being Mr. Popular, but I'm definitely better off than I used to be. Maybe you came from a socially different culture, maybe you struggle with self-esteem, maybe you just don't feel like leaving your comfort zone and making an effort to become friends with everybody you meet. Whatever might negatively affect your desires to put yourself out there and make friends, don't fool yourself into thinking that you're okay without trying.

Being extra friendly to everybody you meet will do nothing but open doors of opportunity for you time and time again. I had a couple of roommates in college who were amazing when it came to meeting new people. Everybody loved them, and they made a sincere effort to become friends with everybody . . . and I mean e-v-e-r-y-b-o-d-y! I subconsciously decided that if I probably wasn't going to be around a person in the future, I wouldn't waste my time becoming acquainted. Looking back, I really regret not making more of an effort. With a career in real estate and financial investing, more friends equals more money. Lots more friends equals lots more money! That shouldn't be your motivation when you're making friends, however. The happiest people on earth are those who enjoy healthy relationships with other people.

It doesn't matter what you plan on doing . . . I guarantee you that having more friends will lead to greater wealth. To have more friends, you need to make a conscious and sincere effort.

While this chapter isn't geared towards explaining the nit-picky details about social skills, it was written to remind you of the importance of not closing yourself up inside a bubble. Even after you're married, meet new people and try to get them to like you. I suggest reading *How to Win Friends and Influence People* by Dale Carnegie. This particular book delves into several concepts that will help you to develop relationships and create lasting impressions. If you have nothing else in this life but friends, you have all you need to succeed.

Subcategories of Social Skills

Happiness, presentation, and communication all fit into the category of social skills. Consistent happiness is so attractive! Acting happy, even when you aren't happy, is an absolute must. Nobody likes a grouch or a whiner! Constant complaining is repulsive while a smiling face and cheerful heart are magnetic.

Also, presentation is a big factor in social situations. As a missionary, you were required to maintain a clean-cut hair style and wear shiny shoes, white shirts, and conservative ties. This was a reflection of the message you were called to preach. How you present yourself to the world usually affects your likelihood for success. I love to wear basketball shorts with a T-shirt, sandals, and my ten-year-old ball cap, but if I were to walk into a meeting with a potential client wearing such an outfit, my chances for success would plummet. Present yourself appropriately if you're concerned about attracting wealth. Not that you need to strut around in a tuxedo to be successful, but an unkempt appearance will certainly repel potential opportunities . . . especially in first-impression situations.

Communication was key in determining how you got along with your companion. If you didn't talk to him and communicate what was on your mind, he would think you were mad at him or didn't like him, which in turn triggered negative thoughts in his mind. He then stopped talking, began harboring bad feelings towards you, and developed a tendency to magnify every little, disagreeable thing you did. After a week or maybe a month of frustration, you let each other have it during companionship inventory. Everything would come out. After realizing that you lost the influence of the Spirit and that the only real problem was a lack of communication, you figured out that vocalizing your thoughts clearly and frequently would help avoid similar conflicts in the future.

Do you think marriage is any different? If you're not to that stage in life yet, here's a little pointer for you: communicate! Those of you who are already there—you know what I'm talking about. Don't just close yourself up and get all upset about something for a couple of days. Having to ask "what's wrong?" ten times over a several day time period before discovering the reason for all the drama just isn't necessary. Being open and honest in a non-hurtful manner will help you achieve greater happiness in your marriage, and greater happiness in your marriage will drive you to succeed in your daily endeavors. Avoid using words like "you always" or "you never" in those little eternal companionship inventories. The focus on marital communication is important here, because having a happy marriage will be a very influential component of your quest for wealth.

Communication obviously applies to the work environment as well. If you can't communicate well to your employees what it is you need them to do, a functional business system will be difficult to achieve. If you can't communicate well with your customers why it is that they should buy from you, guess what! That's right, they probably won't be buying anything from you. Communicating well with business partners will prevent the possibility of destroying a profitable relationship. The applications are endless with communication skills, so evaluate yourself often on how well you're communicating your thoughts and feelings with those around you.

Leadership and Teamwork

More than likely, you learned more than you ever imagined you could during the first couple of months in your mission. Before you knew it, you were training a new missionary, then a small district, then a whole zone of missionaries, and possibly you even worked at the head of the whole mission. You were likely given different responsibilities here and there that required you to lead one or many others in the work. (If not, that's okay! You were called to be a missionary and whether you were a junior companion or an assistant to the president, you were a missionary and equally as important.) While the topic of leadership could very easily be comprehensive enough to fill the pages of several books, suffice it to say that the methodologies and attributes that you developed as an effective leader in the mission field are necessary in whatever you decide to do for a living. If you can apply the skills of directing and inspiring others in any project, you will see tremendous results.

Many opportunities to create wealth come packaged in an attractive combination with teamwork. While I believe that one of the number one rules of business is "if you can do it by yourself, don't complicate things by bringing on partners," most larger-scale investments will require the participation of others. You coordinated with bishops, ward mission leaders, ward missionaries, other full-time missionaries, and members to accomplish great things in the mission. If you can systematically coordinate a team of experience and intelligence, investment capital, and the right skills, the possibility of building enormous wealth is without limit.

For example: One of my companions returned home and obtained a college degree in English. Before graduating, he began working in real estate and was in the business of finding large plots of land for a developer. Now, he works for himself doing the same thing, but he has a team that enables him to form very large and profitable projects. He finds farmers willing to sell their land; one of his partners pays for the land; another partner pays to develop the land; they sell the development and divide the profits between the three. If you'd like to graduate college debt free and with a net worth of around a quarter of a million dollars like he did, remember the concept of teamwork!

Continue the Discipline

Perhaps what will have the most impact on your financial outcome in life will be your ability to discipline yourself. If you could survive two whole years of total consecration and complete obedience to a higher law, it would seem that maintaining a little self-discipline throughout the rest of your life wouldn't be all that tough. Several external influences will help you with your discipline (wife, friends, family, and so forth), but if you can't give yourself a solid kick start every day, just forget about it. If you wouldn't get up on time and do your companionship study as a missionary, you definitely weren't preparing yourself with the Spirit, which meant that you forfeited a certain amount of missionary success. If you're not maintaining a set schedule and making yourself follow an agenda of productivity, you absolutely cannot become rich . . . without miracles.

Discipline yourself to think about ways to obtain money; discipline yourself to act on and carry out good ideas; discipline yourself to concentrate and follow through the several phases of a business venture; discipline yourself to expand and continually increase your net worth (some people happen to obtain a good chunk of change, and then they throw in the towel). Whether you're studying to become a lawyer or saving up every penny to invest in your new widget idea, you will discover very soon that without discipline you can accomplish little.

Overcome Your Defeats

Lastly, reject rejection and don't succumb to failure! Knocking doors is one of the least effective ways of doing missionary work; we've all been there, and we've all suffered one rejection after another. It requires a special personality in this life to face rejection time and time again and not let it slow you down. With a burning testimony to drive you every minute of every day, rejection wasn't so bad as a missionary, but when you're not doing the most important work in the world anymore, rejection hits you in a whole new way. Family members might treat you like a lost lunatic, friends might have pessimistic comments to share about your untraditional ways, or financial "experts" might tell you that you're headed nowhere.

First off, take your financial advice from those with a bank account large enough to show that they know what they're talking about. Learn how to make money from the millionaires that are making the money. Not to say that if they don't have money, they never know what they're talking about, but I've seen worried, caring relatives and close friends try to convince those trying to become wealthy that they will be worse off for trying. That's why 98 percent of the world works for the other 2 percent. The 2 percent are those who don't listen to the multitudes telling them that being different will ruin their future.

Chances are that you will work hard to make something happen financially, and it just won't work out at first. Everybody runs in to a big, brick wall from time to time. Just because it doesn't happen perfectly the first time or you bust after you've boomed for a while, that's no reason to give it all up and decide that you should've listened to grandma and her conventional wisdom. The average millionaire goes bankrupt more than once, so don't allow yourself to think that you won't hit any bumps along the road. Ask Abraham Lincoln and Colonel Sanders about not giving up. They'll tell you in a heartbeat how many failures you have to endure in order to achieve the extraordinary.

You Are Equipped with All the Weapons Necessary

With your arsenal of missionary attributes and work habits, you really are prepared to do absolutely anything. Pick up any book about sales or any book about business and see how many pages you have to read before it dawns on you that you already learned everything it's teaching when you were a missionary. The applications were a little different, but most of the concepts are identical. If you continue to apply the things that helped you be successful in the field, there is no limit on what you can accomplish for yourself and your family in this life.

Exercise:

Write down five skills and attributes that most affected your success as a missionary. Once you've identified these five things, commit them to memory and decide that you will continue to incorporate them into your daily life. Continue to develop the skills and attributes you cultured as a full-time missionary, and integrate them into your financial life fittingly.

NOTE: I'm serious about doing these things. If you aren't doing the exercises or decide that you want to do them another day, this book isn't for you, because the only way to see results is by *doing* . . . not procrastinating!

4

Set Goals and Plan

As mentioned previously, you developed several essential skills and work habits that established a framework for your mission. Undoubtedly, the primary step repeated daily throughout the missionary routine, which ultimately determined whether you'd witness a glorious day or find it rather frustrating, was the act of goal setting and planning. In the book of Proverbs we read, "Where there is no vision, the people perish" (29:18). Now that you've returned home, do you map out your days in advance?

Be a Visionary

I remember the first day in the field with my trainer. After he and his companion picked me up from the mission office the evening before, I spent the entire night wide awake on the concrete floor that served as my new bed. Something wasn't settling right in my stomach, so I madly bolted for the bathroom a few times throughout the night anticipating that I would vomit. (I apologize for including the details, but the story would be a little dry without them.) Good ol' Peru! The first morning, we went and dropped off his companion that I was replacing, and then we headed back to our area to study and plan our day.

I was, of course, super excited about finally being in the field and ready to make a difference. I had been imagining what it would be like for months and naively thought that I had great ideas to baptize mobs of people. My trainer was taken aback a little when I shared with him some of the activities and proselyting methods I thought would be effective, but he appreciated the vigor with which I was ready to serve.

He thanked me for wanting to work hard, and we decided to set our companionship goals for the next month/week/day. It happened to be the day that the weekly reports were to be handed in to our district leader, so we filled those out first. I remember it very distinctly, because we had to draw all of these perfect boxes for the numbers, and if we messed up, we had to start over. Included on the reports was everything that had been accomplished the week before and all of our new goals for the upcoming month and week.

I learned that before we did anything else, we had to define our vision and set a series of goals, which would ensure that we made our vision a reality. By setting monthly goals, and then weekly and daily goals that focused on our monthly goals, we were able to accomplish so much more. Giving structure and organization to our daily efforts was paramount in determining the success we enjoyed.

Two months before that time, I made sure to follow that "early to bed and early to rise" mantra . . . I always went to bed early in the morning (2:00 AM) and woke up early in the afternoon. The only agenda I worried about was making it to work on time and showing up for the dates I had planned. Suddenly, the world of missionary work turned my life upside down, and I witnessed miracle after miracle because of it. Because I lived two years of my life at such a high level of productivity, I will never be able to go back. Understanding the principles of setting goals and planning to execute them is now a part of who I am. Hopefully, you too gained that from your mission experience.

Visionary Goals

I saw firsthand the powerful influence that a clear vision can have on missionary work. The Peru Lima North Mission was full of hard-working missionaries who were truly establishing the Church. Every once in a while, however, a missionary would come along that was able to accomplish more than the other missionaries in the field. While the average companionship would teach twelve discussions a week, another would be working in the armpit of the mission teaching twenty discussions a week.

A peculiar phenomenon took place a couple of times during my two-year adventure. The first happened when the goal of monthly discussions was raised by some motivational zone leaders. The mission-wide expectancy was forty-eight discussions per month or twelve discussions per week for each companionship. These zone leaders were consistently teaching twenty discussions per week and around eighty per month.

One of them was inspired enough to flash his planner in my face and rub it in a little. In a sense, he was challenging me to step up my diligence and start teaching more people. Within two weeks, my companion and I had analyzed our time and planned our schedules in a way that allowed us to finish up a week with twenty-three discussions. I remember dancing around our room, celebrating the fact that we had basically doubled the amount of teaching that we were previously doing. Obviously, when you start teaching more people, you start baptizing more people as well.

Pragmatic Planning

The key to teaching twice as many discussions was in our weekly and daily goal setting. We considered our goals to be promises to Heavenly Father. We promised to do our best to reach the goals we had set, and we prayed every single morning before leaving our apartment that He would help us accomplish the things we had planned. We knew exactly how many hours we had available for teaching and how many minutes it would take to walk from one place to another. We set our goals accordingly and prayed several times a day for the opportunity to reach those goals.

I found myself going from six discussions a week in my first area to over twenty discussions a week in my second area and throughout the rest of my mission. What's interesting though, is that teaching six discussions a week wasn't considered all that bad when I first started the mission. When more missionaries started teaching more discussions, the whole mission raised the bar and started teaching way more than had ever been taught before.

Another incredible experience was the vision we had for baptizing people into the Church. The goal for each companionship in the Lima North Mission was two-with-one for each month. That meant that each companionship could baptize two adults, but that one needed to be a priesthood holder who could accept a leadership position in the Church. Honestly, it was easier for "gringo" missionaries to baptize women and children, but the mission president directed us to search for priesthood leadership and families.

Every month, somewhere in the mission, at least one companionship would turn in reports of eight or nine convert baptisms for that month. This irked me, because I was under the impression that if one companionship could do it, then others could too.

We talked about it in a zone meeting one morning and discussed the possibility of bringing more people into the Church on a monthly basis—just like these other missionaries. We asked five different companionships if they were willing to set a baptismal goal equivalent to what other missionaries had accomplished over the previous four months. As a zone we challenged ourselves to baptize seven-with-four per companionship the next month (that began a week later).

Of the five companionships in the zone, these were the attitudes: 1) it can't be done—we'll shoot for two-with-one; 2) we don't think we can do it—but we'll try; 3) it's a possibility, so we'll do our best; 4) let's do it; and 5) the companionship that presented the idea and obviously shared the vision.

Five weeks passed and reports were turned in. These were the results: Companionship 1: two converts and proud to have reached their goal. Companionship 2: four new converts and surprisingly pleased with their fruits, but a little disappointed that they didn't reach their goal. Companionship 3: seven converts and flabbergasted. Companionship 4: nine solid converts and a whole ward excited about it. Companionship 5: fourteen converts consisting of four different families. With results like this, every companionship in the stake started receiving referrals like crazy. The members wanted missionaries that were baptizing to teach their friends, and the stake grew by leaps and bounds.

Soon, the vision throughout the whole mission changed. The standard goal was raised from two-with-one to four-with-two. The monthly number of converts went up from around two hundred per month to around three hundred per month, and all of it was directly related to our vision of teaching and baptizing. Once the vision changed and missionaries focused on goal setting with pragmatic planning, the Church in Peru saw much stronger growth.

Have a Daily Agenda

By all means, there are missions in the world who baptize much more than this; and there are missions that baptize much, much less. I relate this story to you only to illustrate the point. Productivity goes through the roof when a person knows what he wants to do, he sets goals to do it, and he plans out every hour of every day in an effort to reach those goals. Trying to shoot from the hip (without aiming) will get you nowhere fast in life. Arising every morning with an agenda for the day and specific long-term and short-term goals is a key that you must possess if you wish to unlock the doors to success.

Let's relate these principles to life after the mission. Say you have been home for six months to a year now, have a part-time job, are dating somebody, and college classes are kicking your butt. Time is a commodity that you don't have much of.

First thing's first—know what you want to accomplish. Have a vision . . . just like you did when you were wearing your name tag. A guy who doesn't worry about getting married, who doesn't consider earning an extra buck, and who doesn't know what kind of career to work towards is doomed. Everybody has aspirations, but if you fail to define them and inscribe them on paper, it's just wishful thinking.

Set specific goals periodically. Once a year, you should evaluate where you're at and where you want to go in life and write down what it is you want to accomplish one year, five years, and ten years from now. Where do you want to be? If somebody else can do it, then so can you, so don't limit yourself. If you want to teach English in Taiwan, do it. If you want to win a triathlon, do it. If you want to marry Miss America, wake up. Just kidding with you . . . if I can marry a woman as incredible as my wife, there's hope for everybody!

Clarify your vision, put it on paper, and set it by your bed where you will see it every single night. You will notice in this book that I strongly encourage visual reminders that you can see and think about every day as you go to sleep or wake up. Every month, every week, and every day you will look at your goals and set sub-goals that will help you get there . . . just like a missionary does. This is your life, and you control what it will become!

By mentally mapping out your next day and writing everything down on paper, you can really accomplish a lot more in your day-to-day activities. Just the act of getting it down on paper and knowing *what* you will be doing and *when* is a good measure of your productivity. It's not important that you have every single minute planned out with back-up plan A, B, and C, but you should definitely know how you will spend each hour of your day being productive and accomplishing your goals. Ask yourself on a daily basis, "What can I do tomorrow that will enable me to accomplish my long-term goals? How do my activities relate to what I want in my future?"

You'll be tempted to just get up and go without a written plan, thinking that your routine is what it is and there's no time in-between. Write down your day, every day, and I promise that you will accomplish more than Joe Shmoe who doesn't. Everybody has heard it: "If you fail to plan, you plan to fail." If you get to a point where you feel stuck and depressed, like nothing is going your way, I bet a buffalo nickel that you'll realize you aren't living with a vision and you aren't planning your months, weeks, or days. Do this simple little thing that might take five minutes out of your day, and you will accomplish anything and everything you've ever dreamed of. That's a guarantee.

Exercise:

So don't just sit there. Get started right away. Go grab a pen and a piece of paper right now. Write down at the top One Year, Five Years, and Ten Years. Underneath each one, jot down the things you would like to accomplish and where you see yourself. Take this time to set some major goals that will shape your future. Set some spiritual goals, some financial goals, some health goals, and whatever else you can think of. When you're finished, tack it on the wall in a place you will see it, and think about it daily.

You know how to plan, so go ahead and find a planner notebook or just a sheet of paper where you can list your monthly goals along with weekly and daily plans. The more you think about your goals and plan your days in order to achieve them, the happier you will be. By following this simple routine every year, month, week, and day you will become unstoppable. Anything you want will be yours if you can discipline yourself to define your vision, set goals, and plan.

5

Education

"To you boys I say, get on with your education. When you marry, yours will be the obligation to provide for your family. The world of opportunity lies ahead of you, and education is the key that will unlock that door."[1]

Perhaps you plan on being an entrepreneurial-minded businessman for the rest of your life, or maybe you're planning on becoming a philosophy professor or even an accountant. Either way, prophetic counsel teaches us to obtain as much education as we possibly can in this life. President Gordon B. Hinckley admonished us on several occasions to educate ourselves extensively. Remember why we are here! We made a covenant to come to this earth as a means of obtaining a body and gaining experience that would enable us to grow spiritually and become more like our Heavenly Father. Education is a vital part of God's great plan.

College Is a Great Option

Many who might not have been the best of students in high school oftentimes lack a desire to continue studying in a college environment. They refuse the opportunity to earn a college degree, thinking that it would be too difficult. Others feel that college is too expensive or not really necessary when it comes to finding a good job.

I will point out that college is a great means of self-improvement that will surely lead to no regrets down the road. The only people who graduate from college feeling sorry they ever applied to a university are those who have accumulated a crazy amount of debt that they feel will be impossible to pay back. On the contrary, many who decide against college express the deepest regrets later on in life. I hear it all the time . . . "If I had just finished up my college education, we'd be much better off than we are now. Dropping out was a foolish thing to do."

If your passion in life is journalism, and you've always wanted to be a news reporter, the only way to become one is by seeking out a college education. Most professional occupations will require a college degree if you ever wish to work in a specific field. Many professions these days even require advanced degrees such as a master's or a doctorate.

Whether you plan on using a degree to obtain your dream job, or you have no intentions of ever being somebody else's employee, you should do everything possible to get a college education. You will be more intelligent and dynamic in character after completing the course work for a bachelor's degree.

In all honesty, there's not really much else to do with your time when you get home from the mission. Going to college is probably the best way to put yourself in an environment where you will find your eternal companion. Going to a student ward enables you to build a large social network and grow your dating pool with potential candidates. I knew after my second semester of college that I would never use my degrees, but I was having a blast in the student wards and felt good about learning. I double majored at BYU, earning a degree in linguistics and another in Portuguese. Maybe one day I'll do something with them, but for now they're nothing but a back-up plan in case everything else fails.

If you plan on becoming your own boss, earning a degree gives you a couple of years to experiment with business ideas on the side and figure out exactly what it is you want to do. While the degree might have nothing to do with your ambitions and financial goals in life, it is still a good idea to receive a higher education. I promise you that you will learn things that will help you with money.

The College Experience is Rewarding

The sense of accomplishment and respect that you will receive after graduating from college can do wonders for your confidence. Confidence will be a key factor in determining your financial success in the future. Being a certified and trained professional in any particular field will open up opportunities galore.

You will gain unforgettable experiences and earn lifelong friends. I owe everything I have right now first to my decision to serve a mission, and second, to my college education. It was in college that I met my beautiful wife. It was in college that I associated with some of the finest men and women that walk upon the face of this earth. It was in college that I learned to speak a couple of languages that come in handy almost daily. It was in college that I was inspired to learn about money!

Bag the Excuses and Study for Free

Are you still doubting? The only legitimate excuses I can think of for not going to college would be a learning disability or a lack of means to pay. Unfortunately, I can do nothing to help with a learning disability, but know that many students conquer their disabilities at college and earn a degree regardless. I can, however, explain to you a way that college tuition won't cost you a dime! That's right . . . not one single dime. You're probably thinking, "I'm not scholarship material," but I'm here to tell you that you don't even need a scholarship to have your college education paid for.

This wonderful country has been set up and governed by leaders who understand the importance of a good education. They have provided a means whereby college students can receive a degree without having to pay the costly tuition fees.

Grants

You are more than likely a candidate for what is known as a Pell Grant. They look at several factors to determine whether or not you qualify, but one of the most heavily weighed factors is your parents' tax returns. If your parents are claiming you as a dependent on their taxes, they receive a several thousand dollar tax break and the government will probably not award you a Pell Grant.

In order for your parents to rightly claim you as a dependent, they are required to pay for at least half of all of your living expenses, which includes the cost of tuition. If they are claiming you as a dependent, but they aren't paying for anything, you'll need to talk to them about the situation. When they don't claim you as a dependent, your chances of qualifying for the Pell Grant go way up.

Visit www.fafsa.com to fill out the government paperwork and find out if you qualify. The application takes about an hour to fill out, and you will know what you qualify for within a few days. If you are awarded the Pell Grant, you will receive a check for up to several thousand dollars per semester or enough to cover your tuition and books (sometimes less depending on how much money you earn). And guess what? That money is yours to keep and never pay back. It's free! The only thing it costs you is the time to fill out the application.

You can receive this grant every year until you've reached a certain limit of credit hours on your university transcripts. They don't want you spending this money on classes that aren't necessary to graduate, so they limit your qualification when you surpass the determined amount of hours. In some cases, you can even file for an extension. I happened to need more classes than most students in my studies, so they approved the disbursement of another Pell Grant to me even after I surpassed the credit limit.

In addition to the Pell Grant, there are several other grants available to students in need of assistance. A brief trip to the university's financial aid office can help you know all of your options.

Scholarships

Another way to avoid paying for tuition is to make good grades. My sister and her husband both went to BYU as well. She worked full time and took a full load of classes while he focused 100 percent of his time and energy on his grades, so he could get accepted into the medical school of his choice. Not having a job enabled him to study more and maintain a very high GPA. By earning good grades in his classes, he was awarded scholarships that added up to more money than his wife earned working full time. The university covered his tuition completely *and* paid him for performing well in his classes. This route requires discipline, dedication, and a good brain if it's going to work out.

Also, there are several other scholarship programs in the United States that help students pay for their college education. Many of these programs aren't necessarily looking for straight A students to be recipients. In some instances, you can be awarded a scholarship just for being unique . . . perhaps because you served a mission for two years. Who knows! Do some research and apply for a large number of scholarships. Chances are you'll actually receive one or two!

I won a $4,000 scholarship fresh out of high school because of the fact that I played tennis . . . not for any college teams—I just played the sport and received a scholarship from the USTA because of it. You never know who will send money your way to help pay for your education.

My last semester in school, I not only had all my costs covered by grants, but I was actually paid two thousand dollars extra! Let me be the first to tell you that I was far from a straight A student. Matter of fact, my GPA was an astounding 3.2, which isn't very impressive. That kind of GPA would actually make it a little tough for me to be accepted into a master's program in many universities. But, let me tell you—it was a great feeling going to class and knowing that I was getting paid for it. Make the effort to look for grant money along with scholarships and you will find yourself in a much better financial situation than the average college student who graduates with twenty thousand dollars in debt.

Tuition Reimbursement

Last, there are a tremendous number of jobs available that offer tuition reimbursement. You'll have to explore the different opportunities to earn money while in college, and if you see an attractive reason to take a great paying job that offers benefits such as health insurance and tuition reimbursement, it might be a great way for you to graduate college with a handsome net worth. If it's a job that will serve as a stepping stone for your future career plans and will pay for your tuition, go for it.

A close friend of mine took a finance job at Ernst and Young, and on top of his impressive yearly salary and lunch stipend, they covered his tuition and actually paid him to earn a master's degree during the summer months. He was being paid approximately three thousand dollars each month to obtain his master's while his education was totally free. What a life!

With that said, there's really no excuse for not going to college. Our living prophet has taught us to seek out higher education, and the odds of you attending a university for free are in your favor. Even if you go to school part time and stretch your education out over several years, the important principle is that you are continually educating yourself and becoming a better person. Becoming more intelligent will directly influence your ability to build wealth.

EXERCISE:

If you're not in college, reconsider the decision and at least send out an application or two to a university you'd like to attend. There are colleges that will accept anybody, so don't give up if you aren't admitted at first.

Visit the financial aid office and learn everything you can about how you can pay for your education without borrowing student loans. There are experts who can help you find several different grants, scholarships, or reimbursement programs. Don't forget to fill out the forms at www.fafsa.com.

Note

1. Gordon B. Hinckley, " 'I Am Clean,' " *Ensign*, May 2007, 60–62.

6

Self-Smart

> It is both relaxing and invigorating to occasionally set aside the worries of life, seek the company of a friendly book and mingle with the great of the earth, counsel with the wise of all time, and look into the unlived days with the prophets. Youth will delight in the heroic figures of Homer; or more modern, will thrill to the silent courage of Florence Nightingale on the battlefields. . . . The power of Cicero's oratory may awaken new ambitions in middle age, or the absurdity of Don Quixote riding mightily against a windmill may make your own pretentiousness seem ridiculous; if you think the world is against you, get the satisfaction of walking the streets of Athens with Diogenes, lantern in hand in broad daylight in search of an honest man. . . . *From the reading of "good books" there comes a richness of life that can be obtained in no other way.* It is not enough to read newspapers. . . . But to become acquainted with real nobility as it walks the pages of history and science and literature is to strengthen character and develop life in its finer meanings.[1]

Being able to shape your soul and character by the type of fuel you feed your mind is one of the greatest blessings bestowed upon us. "Yea, seek ye out of the best books words of wisdom; seek learning, even by study and also by faith" (D&C 88:118). Being well-educated gives you a basis for discussion with other educated people. It provides self confidence. It helps you develop skills and intellectual experience for the analysis of the world. Most important, it provides a basis for thinking, and the way you think is the ultimate influence on the way you live.

How Much You Learned as a Missionary

It's a safe bet to say that you are much smarter after returning home than you were before you put on a name tag as a full-time missionary out to convert the world. The first three weeks to three months of your mission were spent at the famous MTC, where you attended approximately twelve hours a day of meetings, classes, and trainings designed to cram your soul full of doctrine, language, teaching skills, and missionary protocol. Twenty-four whole months of at least two to two and a half hours a day of scripture study and missionary education was the foundation of your unforgettable experience.

According to Elder Holland, it's that small window of opportunity to feast upon the words of Christ every morning that makes or breaks a mission![2] Seven-hundred and thirty days with at least two hours scheduled in to study and be taught from on high was some of the most precious and valuable time this life has to offer. It was during this time spent memorizing scriptures, developing your lessons, learning the language, and understanding the pillars of God's kingdom on earth that you developed a burning testimony.

The study session was a precursor that determined the results of the rest of your day. If you did not fill yourself with the Spirit during the morning study time, the rest of your day simply stunk! Those who slept in a little later and didn't take advantage of that sacred appointment with the scriptures denied themselves the success and personal growth that every missionary is entitled to. Mom and Dad weren't there squirting you with a water gun to get you out of the bed. Those who were disciplined enough to follow the rules and comply with the missionary agenda were certainly privileged to become part of conversion after conversion as an instrument in God's hands. The select few who peeled themselves out of bed even earlier than expected in order to study more likewise received an abundance of power from on high to be successful in every aspect of the work.

It was the simple act of educating yourself that determined the caliber of missionary that you became. Every single day depended on you opening up some source of knowledge or wisdom and soaking it in to the best of your ability! If you slacked off on this learning opportunity, you lost a great measure of spiritual power. By soaking in the teachings of good books, you improved your life and others' lives.

Hunger for Knowledge

I'm sorry to inform you that the days of rigorous learning are far from over. The habit of self-education must continue throughout the remainder of your life. President Hinckley encouraged us time and time again to "be smart"![3] Whether you are in an institute of higher learning preparing for a future profession or living comfortably beside a golf course with millions in the bank, the desire to learn must never fade away.

I just don't understand how some are content with never picking up a book to study a topic of value or pausing on the History Channel or the Discovery Channel long enough to take in the smallest fragment of knowledge. The fact that you are reading this book shows that you are headed in the right direction . . . keep it up! A wise man once said, "Knowledge is power!" I'm here to tell you that he was right. We can also conclude that the opposite stands true in that a lack of knowledge is weakness.

I honestly would go nuts if I didn't always have access to knowledge and education. Going to college was great for the most part because I was forced to learn things. While I don't feel like some of the classes I had to take at BYU to receive my degrees were necessary, the overall experience made me a much smarter person. An interesting phenomenon was that when I wasn't actually taking classes during the summertime, I found myself with an insatiable hunger for knowledge that I could only appease by reading stacks of books about things that interested me. Fortunately, money interests me, so I have read quite the library of books written on the subject of money, and this has played a huge role in getting me to where I am today.

Mold Yourself through Education

You don't have to be a genius or the geeky nerd type to develop a need to read. I'm certainly no genius, but I've stimulated my brain with the inspirational teachings found in books in such a way that my personality, character, aspirations, and skills have been molded into a newer and better me. The great thing about life is that we can always improve and better ourselves, and it depends on what information we decide to fill our cerebral bank with.

If you want to be like Joseph Smith, there are fountains of knowledge that will help you understand his character and actions. All it takes is a thorough study about who he was and the life that he lived, and you will surely begin to emulate his personality and his accomplishments. Why do you think we must learn of Christ in order to have faith, which is the primary principle of the gospel? You cannot learn of Heavenly Father or his son Jesus Christ without innately feeling the desire to become like them. Thus, your individuality is molded into perfection.

If you want to live a life like Millionaire Moe, the obvious way for you to make that happen would be to study how Moe accomplished what he did. If you want to become the next Warren Buffet, you should consider picking up his biography and learning what it was that made him the most successful stock investor of all time.

Create Your List of Education

Right now would be a good time for you to grab a pen and a piece of paper and create a list of the following: A) five influential people that you admire and would like to become like; B) five characteristics that you would like to develop (leadership, charm, humility, and so on); C) five financial topics that you need to learn more about (stocks, e-commerce, life insurance, and so forth).

Write down this list and make it a point in your life to educate yourself about the people, the characteristics, and the financial subjects that will help you reach your potential. The most effective way to accomplish this is by collecting books that have already been written about them. It's awesome to realize that you can become like Benjamin Franklin, a man who lived hundreds of years ago. Because his history is preserved in numerous volumes of books, you can know him better than he might have known himself. (Incidentally, he also created lists of attributes he felt he needed to learn about and develop.) Keep your list by your bed, and make it a point to check off each one after you've sufficiently fed yourself with knowledge pertaining to it.

Just as you had to learn mounds of information to become an effective missionary, you must continue to accumulate knowledge about the things you wish to be successful at. You cannot become a great businessman unless you study what it is that made others great businessmen.

Collect Your Personal Library

The public library in your community has more books than you could ever read, and they are just waiting to change your life. It's a great way to save a little money, but if you can splurge on your own copy, I'd suggest building a personal library. Very few of us are lucky enough to have a perfect memory, so it's a good idea to highlight key concepts, underline inspirational teachings, and mark the pages. If I don't pick up a book that I've read before and skim through my notes and marked pages every couple of years, the lessons learned tend to fade away into the forgotten file. If you check out a book from the library, keep detailed notes in a personal notebook.

Study Everything

I firmly believe that life after the mission very closely parallels the experience you had in the field. Just as you absolutely depended on the morning scripture study to merit the Holy Ghost, which was the key to success during your mission, you must enrich your mind and character by soaking up knowledge constantly. If you fail to be self-smart, which is an ongoing process of you taking the initiative to learn new things, the odds of becoming successful are not in your favor. It doesn't always need to be books about money. You'd get tired of reading pretty quick if every day was the same topic. Exploring books that teach you a variety of subjects such as how to build a house from top to bottom, astronomy, fishing, world history, or even tennis could change your life.

There was a farmer named Robert Landers not too long ago who decided one day that he wanted to learn how to whack a golf ball around in his cow pasture. He got a bucket of balls and some clubs and began practicing his swing during his spare time. Pretty soon, he realized that he had found a new hobby.

In 1995, his newly discovered talent landed him a career on the professional golf senior tour. He was the only golfer you'd see on the course with tennis shoes and blue jeans—he wasn't the number one pro, but he was able to play professionally for a few years and earn enough money to pay off his house and all of his debts. Playing golf cut out several years of hard work that it would've taken to pay everything off at the rate he was going. It also paid him enough to set up a lifestyle that would never require him to go into debt again. Just the willingness to learn a small hobby, and learn it well, altered his life for the better.

I know this is a Cinderella story, but you never know how the knowledge you obtain will play a role in building your financial dreams. The world is full of learning adults who turn their hobbies into lucrative careers every day. Some become artists who sell their paintings for hundreds of thousands of dollars while others put on gardening seminars to share their abundant expertise about mother nature for free. Many convert their knowledge into books and enjoy the royalties from each copy sold for the rest of their lives.

Knowledge and Education Are Priorities for Those Who Understand Life

Did you know that most people who go through a near-death experience come back with a whole new outlook on life? They almost universally find a new focus on two things in particular: relationships and education. These people that receive a sneak peak into the other side of the veil realize upon waking up that the only two things they'll be taking with them are their relationships and their knowledge. That's right—the money stays here. But, again, that doesn't mean you're wasting your time by trying to accumulate wealth. It's part of God's plan that you work to provide for your family, and nowhere did He say that you shouldn't try to be successful at providing for the people you love.

Education Leads to Success Which Leads to Freedom

By efficiently creating wealth for yourself and your loved ones, you free up your time to accomplish greater things. Those who have effectively established their household often find themselves more involved in politics, trying to make the world a better place for their kids. Others serve one mission after another in all parts of the world—growing much closer to their spouses and Heavenly Father. Imagine being a missionary all over again with the love of your life. I can't think of anything that I look forward to more.

This world has so much to offer for somebody with the means to take advantage of the abundant opportunities. There is nothing wrong with working until you're sixty-five and waiting to free yourself from the rigors of a full time job. Personally, though, I want to enjoy the freedom of retirement several years before then, so I can get out and do things more appealing and more productive than trying to earn a paycheck. It is knowledge that will enable us to do this! Knowledge equals options.

Knowledge Allows You to Become Whatever You Want

The self-smarts that you acquire throughout life will enable you to choose whatever means you find most favorable to produce an income. You might opt for the quickest route that requires the least amount of energy to earn your wages while others will simply opt for the activity that brings them the most enjoyment. I had a neighbor growing up who loved to fish. He always said, "Do what you love most and the money will come." If he (and many others) could earn a living by fishing every day, you can find a way to earn a buck doing pretty much anything you can imagine.

Suggested Readings

In conclusion, here is a small list of very influential books that can teach you things essential to your future success. I highly recommend you find a copy and read them:

Multiple Streams of Income by Robert Allen
Multiple Streams of Internet Income by Robert Allen
The Millionaire Next Door by Thomas J. Stanley and William D. Danko
How to Win Friends and Influence People by Dale Carnegie
The Richest Man in Babylon by George S. Clason
Think and Grow Rich by Napoleon Hill
The Automatic Millionaire by David Bach
Rich Dad, Poor Dad by Robert Kiyosaki
The Cash-flow Quadrant by Robert Kiyosaki and Shannon Lechter
Missed Fortune by Douglas R. Andrew
The E-myth Revisited by Michael E. Gerber
The Twenty-One Indisputable Qualities of a Leader by John C. Maxwell
Time Power by Brian Tracy
Any real estate or stock market investment books

These books contain basic ideas and theories you need to be aware of during your quest for abundance. The principles and fundamentals will help guide you in the right direction and can illuminate the way as you take the first steps. Remember to *use* the knowledge that you acquire . . . don't rush into investments frantically, but know that learning everything there is to know about money will do you absolutely no good unless you apply your knowledge constructively. Also, many want to understand every jot and tittle before they make any moves. Most of your successful endeavors will only be fully understood after you've commenced, so don't let an incomplete knowledge hold you back. The only way to truly gain the experience and know-how is by *doing*.

Exercise:

As soon as you finish this book, have another one ready to begin. I suggest finding one from the list provided in this chapter, but any book written on a topic that you wish to learn about will work fine. Keep track of how many books you read each year from here on out. One a month is a good start, but hopefully you'll begin reading as many as one a week. The more you read and study, the more your ability to succeed will increase.

Notes

1. Sheri Dew, *Go Forward with Faith: The Biography of Gordon B. Hinckley* (Salt Lake City: Deseret Book, 1996), 72–73; emphasis added.
2. Mission President Seminar, "*Missionary Work and the Atonement,*" June 20, 2000.
3. Gordon B. Hinckley, *Way to Be!: 9 Ways to be Happy and Make Something of Your Life* (New York: Simon & Schuster, 2002), 25.

7

Dating and Fun

Now that you're safe to be alone with members of the opposite sex, it's time to consider a few pointers about dating and fun when you return from a mission. While this book is not strictly limited to men, this chapter is aimed toward the brethren out there. You might be intrigued by a section about dating in a book concerning the accumulation of money, but what is covered here might be the single most essential lesson in this book.

No Dating = No Marriage

An important tip I can give you is to balance life and prioritize your goals. I never had any intentions of attending BYU after returning home from Peru, but a burning desire to marry a righteous young woman led me to seek out a more abundant marketplace. Being from a town with a population of twenty-five hundred in southeast Texas and in a stake that took four hours to drive across, I was convinced that the pickings were slim. Six weeks of relaxation and being with my family was all I needed before I packed my bags, jumped in my Dad's station wagon, and moved to Utah. It was time to start hunting!

What I mean by prioritize is this: throughout the course of any given day, you study, work, play, sleep, and eat. You'll find that it's near impossible to actually do all of those during a day. Some choose not to sleep; some choose not to work and opt to live off of loans; others don't study and flunk their classes.

Those with their priorities a little out of whack choose not to play, and what I mean by not playing is not dating. They claim they don't have time, because classes are too tough, the job is too demanding, and playing college ball doesn't leave any free time to get to know somebody. Don't be dumb! I don't care what degree you're working on, what kind of classes you're taking, or how many hours of sleep you're getting . . . what you better be doing is searching for your eternal companion. Take a minute to read through the Proclamation to the World that explains the importance of families if you're in doubt.

Don't Procrastinate Marriage

Some mistakenly believe that a man should obtain an education and become financially stable before committing to marriage. I'm here to tell you that nothing could be further from the truth. Whether you marry ten months after your mission, or ten years later, you'll never truly be ready. Have faith that God will take care of you. We're never 100 percent ready to do these sorts of things, but *you cannot procrastinate covenants with the Lord.*

Remember those investigators who knew the Church was true and understood that they needed to be baptized but wouldn't commit? They always thought that they should wait a while until they felt completely ready and really understood everything. Did you agree with them, or did you help them realize that the requirements for baptism were just faith and repentance? The idea of being sealed for time and all eternity in the temple causes some returned missionaries to be fearful and lean towards postponement. Please understand that when searching for that special someone, you date long enough to know, and you're engaged long enough to be polite (in other words, give the mother-in-law time enough to plan a decent reception).

Your Spouse Will Probably Influence Which Career You Choose

What you do for the rest of your life and how much your income will be is largely determined by the person you marry. If you think you'd like to be an agent for the CIA, because you learned a foreign language in your mission and always thought it would be fascinating work to live as a spy, your wife and family might think otherwise! Would you give up the perfect companion for a job? I wouldn't be surprised if some of you are thinking "yes" or "she would love me no matter what." Even though you always thought you were going to do what you wanted to do, you could be surprised to find out that plans change when you meet the person you're going to marry.

Sometimes you don't meet that special someone until you've already begun a career, which is okay. I'm just saying that marrying the right person is priority number one, and career selection will likely be influenced by that person.

How Picky Should You Be?

Seeing that getting married and starting a family is so central to Heavenly Father's plan, don't waste any time. Date and date right! How do you marry the person for you? Well, for starters, know who *you* are and realize now that you are not perfect. Many come up with a long list of qualities and attributes that they want to check off during a first date of celestial evaluation.

Sadly, many people pass up Mrs. Right because they are too busy looking for Mrs. Perfect. News flash: no such thing as Mrs. Perfect! Now don't take this as a suggestion that settling for less than what you deserve is okay. You deserve somebody amazing and by all means you should set your sights high . . . just not too high.

It's a Numbers Game

Go on as many dates as possible and try to get to know several potential candidates. Some gung ho missionaries, knowing their duty is to get married, rush into a relationship within weeks or even days of returning. Case in point: during the last testimony meeting I attended, a returned missionary bore his testimony and mentioned he had been home for less than two months as he pointed out his fiancée in the congregation. Take your time and explore personalities before committing to an exclusive relationship or buying an engagement ring for anybody.

I don't wish to encourage leading anybody on or giving multiple girls the wrong idea. Be open with the girls you date, and let them know that you enjoy spending time with them and getting to know them better. They should understand that, at first, you are developing a friendship with them that could potentially evolve into romance. During the friendship phase, it is okay to befriend several others as well. Being able to compare and measure your options is preferable to immediate exclusivity with the first or second person you meet.

Again, your concern is to find a wonderful companion as soon as reasonably possible, so don't take the dating game too lightly. At the same time, don't stress out about it too much. It might take years of consistent dating to meet the person you will spend all eternity with. As long as you're actively pursuing, things will fall into place sooner or later.

A little side note on getting a first or follow-up date: don't be afraid to bring a simple flower and let a girl know that you're sincerely interested. Many young men try the non-threatening best friend role, where they pretend not to be romantically forward until the girl flashes a big green light. This is ineffective and confusing at best. Be bold and confident. Get phone numbers and call to ask out . . . text messages are a form of non-committal conversations that sometimes demonstrate fear. Asking for dates through text messages or emails is cowardice! Very rarely does a man who communicates that he is afraid of a girl end up winning her heart.

Well-rounded Dating

Make sure your date activities are well-planned, fun, and reveal personality. Being a gentleman who opens a lady's door, pays several compliments, and knows how to have a good time will certainly conquer a heart more easily than being a boring dud. If your dates are well-coordinated and exciting, the chances of getting a second date go way up.

Just in case locking your heart on the mission has caused acute memory loss, I thought it would be a good idea to include some nice date ideas. I loved to make sure that the activities were fun and set up in three to four stages. If I liked the girl, I'd take her through all the possible stages of the date. If not, it was easy to call it a night early and bring her home. Of course, that only works if you keep the date plans a secret. Just let the girl know how she should dress without telling her exactly what you're going to do . . . that builds suspense too! It was also convenient for me to ask somebody out for a Thursday night so that if things went well, I could ask her out again for the weekend.

Another advantage to having top-notch activities planned means that you can have fun even if you're on a date that isn't going so well. If you're doing something you enjoy, it lightens up an awkward situation that might arise if your personalities aren't meshing too well. If you find that you enjoy each other's company, the girl will connect the feelings and emotions of the fun activity with you, which practically guarantees you another date if you want one.

Ideas: Active dates really help bring out personality . . . if there is any. I realize that many of the following ideas might be limited by your geographical region, but you can always improvise. Choose one, two, or more ideas, and start asking out! Be careful not to create "marathon dates" that are more than three or four hours long unless you're certain that she wants to spend that much time with you.

- Campfire with pizza on a sandy beach where you can hit golf balls dipped in glow stick liquid out into a lake or clearing (just cut open the glow sticks and empty the liquid into a bowl to roll the balls in).
- A fun center where they have inflatable games and obstacle courses.
- Rock climbing or obstacle course where you can help each other through challenging setups.
- Exotic or foreign food restaurants are really fun (let each person choose what the other will eat to spice things up a little).
- Rafting, canoeing, or tubing down a river or in a pond.
- A candlelight dinner on a boat in a lake.
- Find a place where you can have a private, candlelit dinner and dance to a custom CD that you prepared. Bring a laptop in case you want to watch a movie afterwards.
- Go shopping and create a dessert together that you have to eat with no forks, spoons, or hands . . . mouth only!
- Go to a Goodwill store and have each person takes $5 to pick out an outfit that the other person has to wear for the rest of the date.
- Rollerblading somewhere that has beautiful scenery (like a mountain trail in the fall).
- Find anything to do outdoors when you can *enjoy the seasons and weather*: go find a place to paint each other's portrait when the fall leaves are changing colors; have a picnic and go fishing in a stream when the spring flowers are blooming (set everything up beforehand and surprise her with the picnic as you "go for a walk"); go ride Jet Skis out on the open lake when the summer sun is blazing; sled down a fun hill when the winter snows are dumping.
- Flower power . . . don't forget it! Every girl likes flowers because

they make her feel pretty.

- Prepare a scavenger hunt with romantic clues all over town that lead up to a grand finale that's sure to sweep her off her feet (scavenger hunts aren't my favorite because too many people do them, but they can be effective with some creativity).
- Set up a tent with a couch inside it and after cooking over a campfire, watch a movie on a laptop inside the tent . . . dancing by the campfire is another good option.
- Go horseback riding and shoot clay pigeons or targets at a shooting range.
- Find a downhill road or trail where you can use a longboard. Sit together and steer with your bottoms and feet (Provo Canyon has a trail that's perfect for this).
- Play board games together . . . I recommend cheating to see what kind of a reaction you can get out of your date (beware of those who get angry over simple games).
- Go to a fireside or watch general conference with a date, but be careful not to confuse the influence of the Holy Ghost with feelings for the other person.
- Go golfing but tie up your hands and feet so that you have to hop everywhere.
- Road trips are good after you've established a relationship . . . most people I know that went on road trips for a few days with a person they were dating either broke up or decided to get married, so it's a real make-it-or-break-it kind of idea.
- Find a way to help out the needy or the homeless: cook some hotdogs that you can hand out, or donate some clothes. It's a great way to find out how Christlike the person you are interested in really is.
- Play night games like Capture the Flag, Kick the Can, or Mafia.
- Play Frisbee Golf, but create your own course. I did it on the BYU campus; we'd compete against another couple to see who could hit certain statues in the least amount of throws.

- Go to concerts, comedy shows, plays, or musicals.
- Anything formal where the girl can get dressed up is a good way to add some excitement to a date . . . ladies love to dress fancy.

The list could go on, but you get the idea. Be spontaneous and original. You're sure to impress your date and get to know her when you plan a fun evening.

Watching a movie makes it really difficult to get to know somebody, so try to avoid this kind of date until you are well-acquainted with each other and just want to spend time together. Alone time is great, but can also be dangerous. Control your physical intimacy and avoid excessive kissing. You know and understand the law of chastity well, so there's no need for a sermon.

Be Patient When It Comes to Physical Intimacy

Make sure that conversation is upbeat and abundant well before you cross over onto the kissing side of the dating game. Many people kiss too soon and then figure out that they don't really have much to say to each other. What do you think they do next? That's right—they just keep kissing so that they don't have to talk. Before they know it, they have a purely physical relationship that will lead to nothing but trouble. "Parking" alone to engage in kissing can also push the limits, so steer away from this kind of situation (pun intended). Last, gentlemen, between your date's legs is not an appropriate place to find yourself. It doesn't matter if it's an innocent back massage or harmless cuddling on the couch . . . do not allow this position into your dating life (especially when kissing).

Get Your Butt Out There and Create Some Sparks

I find that many guys have theories about "how to get the girl." Don't waste your time philosophizing about whose strategy is the best. Everybody is unique and will fall in love in his or her own special way. It's more useful to go visit people and make new friends than it is to sit and chat with a bunch of single guys about the best way to make a relationship happen. It's just too ironic to be having a conversation on the topic when not one person is walking the walk.

My roommate and I used to discuss and analyze our dates before we went to bed. It was hilarious trying to convince each other of the best way to have a girl fall in love with you. My good friend decided he was going to go ahead and apply my quirky techniques on his next date, and it went horribly wrong. He ended up telling a girl that she had monkey toes and hadn't evolved very well. What's funny is that she really didn't want to go on another date with him but was talked into it by a third party. Now they are happily married and have two children. I must have known what I was talking about. But, then again, my strategy didn't work so well for me! It took me another two years before I tied the knot.

A Spouse Might Be Your Most Influential Factor in Determining Success

In the book *The Millionaire Next Door* by Thomas J. Stanley and William D. Danko, a study was done to compare and contrast stereotypical millionaires in America. One of the most influential factors in a person's financial success is the person he marries. It has to do with the spending habits of your spouse. If you marry a high-maintenance, spoiled-rotten money spender, forget about building a fortune.[1]

On a more spiritual note, you need to marry a person worthy of inviting blessings into your life. Like Joseph of Egypt, God prospers those who earnestly obey his commandments. I have seen God's hand in my financial situation, and I openly attribute a large portion of our prosperity to the spiritual beauty of my wife. She is an angel, and I know God has helped us along because of that.

Napolean Hill, author of *Think and Grow Rich,* taught that a man will be successful because of his love for a woman.[2] If he loves her, he will do whatever it takes to make her happy and provide for her. Call it showboating if you will or being the alpha male.

I had several female friends while in the dating phase of my life and heard on various occasions about the "money potential" that a guy possessed. They would measure a fellow up and analyze his potential ability to earn money in life. You better believe that they considered it a big plus. I hope that no woman is ever attracted to a man based purely on his "money potential," but I know it happens. Money and security is attractive! Guys instinctively know this and feel a subconscious desire to perform well financially in order to provide for their spouses.

My father-in-law's only words of advice when I asked for his daughter's hand in marriage were about money. He said, "My dad always told me that when poverty comes in the door, love goes out the window!" This might not be true all of the time, but I sure don't want to test anything.

Economic Pressure to Perform

You will realize that with marriage comes economic pressure. Your wife will want you to be the breadwinner for the family so that she can raise the children as a full-time mom. There will be bills to pay . . . an overwhelming amount of bills to pay. It starts off with about five to ten bills that you pay each month but soon goes up to twenty to thirty. Usually, the more money you earn, the more checks you'll be writing out each month. Things that you might not have really put much thought into before will spring up once you're married. I know I never thought about paying for health insurance, furniture, vehicles, vacation trips, and so on. Getting married opened up a whole new financial dimension that I had never been responsible for previously.

Nothing will inspire a man to action like the economic pressure I write of. When you know that whether you can afford food, clothes, transportation, and even entertainment depends on you finding a way to earn money, you will step up to the challenge.

My mentality about money wasn't altered by my marriage, but my motivation certainly was. I had several money-making ideas I was packing around in my thick head, but there was no real urgency for me to act on any of them. Once I knew I was getting married though, the switch was flipped, and I found some great ways to increase our income.

I estimate that I augmented my income over 800 percent within the first twelve months of being married . . . and I was still a student! My wife and I sat down a couple of months before our temple date and mapped out all of our expenses that we would be responsible for. Then, we compared the total to our current wages and saw that we would be a few hundred dollars short every month. It would've been easy to opt for student loans until we graduated, but we chose not to increase our debt. I began to apply the concepts of business and investing because of the economic pressure of a married life that we couldn't afford. The results were phenomenal!

In summary, marriage to the right person could very well be the single most important factor that will influence your financial destiny. You will work hard to establish monetary stability, because you love your wife. You will find ways to create wealth because there is an immense pressure ever whispering to you the consequences of failure. God will prosper you because of your righteousness that you share as a family. As a team, you will encourage, teach, and support each other towards your goals of wealth. I want you to be rich, and I happen to know that whether this happens will largely depend on the person that you marry, so date right and marry right. That doesn't mean that marriage is necessary before prosperity, but it sure helps. Good luck in your exciting—and possibly frustrating—adventures of dating!

Exercise:

Meet at least one new person every week that you can add to your dating pool. If this means you have to go swing dancing downtown to meet new faces, then learn some moves and be brave enough to ask for a phone number. Along with meeting one new person every week, go on at least one date every week. Sometimes you can feel down after going on so many dates and not clicking with anybody, but don't let that deter you. One date a week . . . no excuses! If you are already married, same advice—one date a week (with your wife of course). A happy marriage is the best fuel for a productive life.

Note

1. Thomas J. Stanley and William D. Danko, *The Millionaire Next Door* (New York: Longstreet Press, 1988), 36–37.
2. Napoleon Hill, *Think and Grow Rich,* 221–24.

8

Concepts of Business

You've been surrounded by thousands of businesses throughout your life. The world thrives and survives on the basic business model of buying, selling, and trading. There are very few genres of business: sell a product, sell a service, or sell both together. By understanding the essentials of a typical business, you will have more capacity to begin your own successful venture.

Product

Products are usually pretty simple to understand. Neighbor Ned had a widget idea and invented a foot pedal toilet flusher. It's nicer than touching a handle at the top of the toilet: you can avoid wiping your potty germs on it and the countless previous users' germs. It's also a more attractive option than the costly light sensor automatic toilet flushers. The world would become a much better place with toilets that flush at the tap of a foot!

Soon, Ned filed for a patent on his bright new idea and found a way to mass produce his toilet pedal. He found a factory in Venezuela that could make his product at the rate of one thousand per day and a cost of $1.00 each. Neighbor Ned realized that he was on to a huge idea that could really take off, but in order for the Venezuelan pedal factory to make the production worth their time, they required a minimum order quantity (m.o.q.) of sixty thousand units on the first round.

After filing for his patent and scraping together his spare savings that he accumulated from his job at the post office, neighbor Ned realized that he was short to the tune of $40,000. He first tries to convince his rich neurosurgeon brother-in-law to lend him $20,000, which worked out all right. He then went to his dad, his grandma, his neighbors, and anybody else that might have some spare cash, telling them about the fortune he was about to make off of toilet pedals. He probably could've saved himself a lot of trouble by getting a small business loan from a local bank, but friends and family charge lower interest rates on loans, so he pitched his idea to every one of them before he started the venture.

Neighbor Ned put in the purchase order with the factory in Venezuela and they said he will receive all sixty thousand toilet pedals in a freight container three months later. This gave Ned plenty of time to set up shop for his new business. He still worked at the post office full time, but every night he dedicated a few hours to building his website, preparing his advertising, perfecting his marketing plan, running numbers, building out his new location, and so forth.

Three months had come and gone in no time, and Ned found himself with a small warehouse full of toilet pedals. Luckily, he had already gone to several department stores and let them know about his wonderful new product that would revolutionize the way people go to the bathroom. Several orders had already been placed, and the majority of his new widgets were shipped out as soon as he received the container load. He bought his toilet pedals for $1.00 each but sold them to distributors for $3.50 each. All of the stores he sold them to put them on the shelf with a price tag of $6.99 each. They sold, they sold, and they're still selling.

Ned has to expand the production of his toilet pedals due to the high demand. He finds a factory in Pakistan that can make the toilet pedals with a much more durable material and for only 65 cents each. He is even able to sell them to the stores for $4.00 each because of the extremely high demand for this new product. Every distributor that sets up to do business with Ned is able to make good money. He builds a fortune over the next couple of years. His product is still the most effective and economical option for flushing toilets in the world. Thanks to his patent, the toilet pedal is only produced by his company, Foot Flush, and he sets everything up to where his managers and employees run the show while he goes golfing at the country club by the lake.

Ned sells about 750,000 toilet pedals per year, but has only tapped into the market on the West Coast. His company plans on expanding within the next six months and estimates that orders will go up to over two million toilet pedals per year. This means that neighbor Ned doesn't work at the post office anymore! He learned the concept of buying a product for a low price and then marking that price up so he can see a profit off of his investment of time, money, and energy.

In this example, Ned was the manufacturer of his own idea. You do not have to be Thomas Edison to make good money in this life. The majority of people that are in the business of selling products aren't the inventors nor the manufacturers . . . they're the distributors. Most products are sold this way: there's a mass producer who sells to a middle man who sells to the public (many products pass through several middle men). Business sells to business that sells to shoppers. You've heard of wholesale and retail. Wholesale is the price that the distributors pay the manufacturer for the product while retail is the price that the store shoppers pay the distributors.

The concept is the same whether you're buying a toilet pedal, an eraser, or a house. Buy cheap and sell for a higher price. This is how a product-driven business makes money. I know you're thinking, "Well, duh!" right about now. But if you can see and understand this process then you can absolutely make it happen.

A legitimate and prosperous business needs only to find a wholesaler that produces something in mass quantities and will sell it to you (usually in bulk orders) at a price low enough for you to mark up around 30 percent. That means if you can buy it for $100 you should be able to sell it for around $130 or more to make it worth your investment. If you can do the manufacturing yourself and cut out the middle men, then naturally, you're cost will be lower and your profit margins will be higher.

If buying a product at wholesale and selling at retail means you need to scrimp and save for a little while, borrow from your grandma, or go to a bank for a small (or large) loan—do what it takes. When done right, selling products can be an easy and fast accumulation of cash.

Always keep your eye open for a good deal. The trick to making money in anything is when you buy . . . not when you sell! Buy low, and selling will be much quicker and more profitable. I still buy stuff on the side all of the time to pick up some extra cash.

There are "for sale" ads everywhere you go. People buy things and for different reasons decide they don't want them anymore, so they let them go for a steal of a deal. I've bought golf clubs, dogs, TVs, beds, tables, projectors, cars, aquariums, and all kinds of other things just so I could turn around and sell them the next week for a handsome profit. The only way to do this is by studying the product and its market (whether used or new) and jumping on a good price before somebody beats you to it.

Unfortunately, this week I lost an opportunity to earn an extra $400 for about twenty minutes of my time. A lady had a big screen TV she wanted out of her house. It would've easily fetched around $600, but she wanted to get rid of it quick, so she posted an ad for $150. By the time I saw it, somebody else had already called to reserve it, but she almost let me come anyway if I could get it out of her home any quicker than the other caller. She said, "If they don't come, I'll call you tomorrow and you can have it for free. I just want it gone!" This attitude is rampant, and if you hunt for the no-wanters, you can certainly earn some significant cash.

I also buy houses in the same way, but since the investment is much larger, so are the profits. Just this year I bought a duplex that is worth about $50,000 more than what I paid for it. I also bought a home from a couple going through a divorce and a judge mandating that they have the house sold by a certain deadline. I walked into this deal with an immediate $30,000 in equity! Whether I make $50, $500, or $50,000, I'm ecstatic about turning what money I have into a lot more!

Learn how to do this and I guarantee you that in one month you can turn $100 into more than what you would make working full time at a typical student job . . . in other words, you can buy and sell things for just a couple hours a week and realize more earnings than you would slaving away forty hours per week. Find a decent paying job that you can work part time while you buy and sell on the side. You will be amazed at how much money you can receive from your sales profits.

Buying people's junk is more along the lines of running a pawn shop, but it's the same concept no matter what you're dealing with or how you look at it. If you can spot a deal and act quickly, you can make a lot of money.

It's much easier to find one product or a conglomerate of related products to buy from wholesalers and sell in your retail location. Some decide to specialize in just doors while others make a business out of selling everything you could possibly want to build a home. The limit is only your willingness to get out there and find wholesale pricing.

My brother began buying and selling things while he was still in college. He graduated with a degree in business, but long before he finished his studies, he was making more money than most professionally employed people twice his age. Needless to say, he not only graduated debt free but had a large sum of money in his bank account. He found a hobby he enjoyed and learned a little about it. After figuring out the concept of buying low and selling for a profit, it didn't take him long to find wholesale suppliers and set up a website that launched his products into the nationwide market of consumers. He now has multiple websites and is extremely successful.

The average college graduate finishes his degree with $20,000 of student loan debt. This is because it's very difficult to go work at a restaurant or telemarketing office and earn enough to pay for tuition, books, rent, transportation, food, dates, and so forth. You don't have to graduate with debt if you can grasp the concept of buying and selling a product.

Service

Another form of business is selling a service: landscaping, haircuts, window washing, entertainment, tutoring, medicine, or belly-dancing lessons. The list is endless. Many people get their college education in providing a service. Some study psychiatry, so they can service people by analyzing their emotional problems and providing counsel. Others go to physical therapy school, so they can provide a service of helping people regain health when they are sick or involved in an accident. Many learn how to frame houses, so they can sell their services to a general contractor for $11.00 an hour, while others learn how to play basketball and sell their services and talents to an NBA team for millions of dollars per year.

The difference between marketing a product and marketing a service is usually how you invest. To market a product, you need to buy it first and then mark the price up as explained earlier. To market a service, you have to obtain the knowledge, skills, and experience to perform that service, which most of the time requires money to pay a teacher or a mentor and a large amount of time dedicated to studying or obtaining experience.

Doctors earn a great wage because, to become one, they invest years and years on education, which can cost hundreds of thousands of dollars. Due to the demanding nature of preparing for a medical profession, few capacitate themselves on the subject, but those who do can charge well for their services. Why? Supply and demand. Hopefully, you already understand this universal concept of economics. If there aren't many doctors, the demand is high, which means you pay more for them to prescribe your medications. A lot of doctors would mean less of a demand and lower consultation fees.

Many service-oriented businesses are governed by licensing laws that ensure you are actually qualified to provide a certain service. In Utah you cannot install a swimming pool unless you have a swimming pool contractor's license. I learned this the hard way, because this was one of my first attempts to start my own business. In my home state of Texas, you can build just about anything without having to obtain a license beforehand, so I assumed that Utah was the same. After months of laying the groundwork for my business, I hit a brick wall that stopped me dead in my tracks. A Utah swimming pool contractor's license required a minimum of two years of experience working underneath a licensed contractor, which I didn't have.

If you'd like to offer a service for your business, make sure you have all the proper documentation for the job. Licensing laws are designed to protect the public, and they ultimately benefit you as well. The requirements usually help make sure you are well-experienced and knowledgeable before receiving permission to operate your own service business. If you're interested in a service where you see a profitable future, do your research, know the laws, and do what it takes to earn the necessary documentation as soon as possible.

Products and Services Together

At times, a combination of products and services offered together in the same business is the best scenario for earning a paycheck. Plumbers wouldn't make it very far if they didn't sell their own hot water heaters. Lowe's and Home Depot wouldn't own the market in their niche if they didn't offer service professionals to install the fences, the windows, the carpet, and everything else they have on their shelves. If you can set up a business, you should have no problem incorporating both products and services where possible and profitable.

The Major Steps of Opening Your Own Business

Getting Started:

Now that you know how to offer a product or a service for a profit, the trick is to choose the right product or service that will earn you the largest sum of money in the shortest time frame . . . and it's probably a good idea to choose something you enjoy. Personally, I'm happy no matter what I'm doing as long as I'm making good money for my time and effort. If I'm sitting behind a nice desk in an air conditioned office making $1000/day

I'm happy. If I'm out in the hot sun, drenched in sweat, wearing a hard hat, and digging holes for $1300/day, I'm happier. Would I do that forever? Nope! But, I'd certainly work hard now if it meant that I could play more a few years down the road.

Judging your target market and your competition is crucial once you've figured out that you're ready to be a business. If you have a product that seems really neat, but it's not very practical and only people from Mongolia would ever find it useful, your target is too small to start up a business. If you have a product that seems really neat and everybody in Mongolia, China, and Russia would buy it, but there are twelve other companies that have been specializing in the same product and marketing them to the same target for the last ten years, you should reconsider your options. Find a product or a service that would be in high demand and make sure the market isn't saturated by too many other companies selling the same thing.

If there are other companies marketing your product idea, only do it if you can offer a better product, better prices, or you're certain that you can outmarket them with superior advertising. Also, be aware that some products are patented by other companies, meaning that you can't sell the same thing unless they give you permission to. The general rule is that a product must be 10 percent different from the patented version if you wish to avoid infringement. I say it's best to stay away from the danger zone and avoid any unnecessary lawsuits that could drain your capital. Visit the following website to do a patent search and seek professional help if you are uncertain about anything: www.uspto.gov.

Name Your Business:

Once you've brainstormed a business idea, identified a promising target market, and checked for patents and trademarks, it's time to put a name on your idea and register your business. A business name should be short, descriptive, easy to spell, and catchy. As discussed in the e-commerce chapter, you will want to verify that the Internet domain for the name you have chosen is available through www.godaddy.com (if the .com domain is taken and they encourage you to buy the .org, .net, or .biz domain, don't do it . . . you don't want to lose any traffic to the other .com domain you don't own). In case you didn't know, .com is short for commerce (knowledge is power, right?).

Examples of effective business names: Lovesac (foam bag furniture),

Kneaders (bakery), Memories (photography), and Comp USA (computers). Many choose a more abstract name like Google or go with a personal name like Larry's Lube, and they perform just as well or better than those with the most original names. This goes to show that the real secret doesn't always lie in the name you choose but the way you market your name.

Business License:

After filtering through possible names, it's time to go to the city hall and pay for your business license. This usually costs between $20 and $100. You will also need to register your name with the state (another fee ranging from $20 to $100). They can tell you where to do this as you apply for your license with the city. There are multiple city regulations and zoning standards that must be followed by commercial businesses, so the application basically tells the city what you're up to, where you'll operate, and the nature of your business. They'll make sure you understand different laws about signage, parking, storage, employees, fire codes, and maybe a few other details.

Tip: I suggest registering a business license sooner rather than later. When you arrive to a point where you wish to find commercial loans, the lenders usually want to see at least two years of business history. The first thing they do is perform a search on your business license to determine the date you began. It might be beneficial to have the business registered before it is fully operational . . . this doesn't mean, however, to register a license for any whim of an idea before it is planned and you know it will be profitable.

Location:

Choose a wise location for your business. Don't be afraid of a lease that costs a little bit more if it is going to bring in way more customers than the place that costs half as much but is hidden from view. Also, do your best to make sure your business idea will actually work before you sign a contract for a location (you can usually find temporary leases for trial runs).

I recently had the opportunity to buy a tanning salon business that was totally remodeled with over $75,000 invested into it. The owner was asking $15,000 because of health issues and insurance problems, which I thought was an amazing bargain. I started watching the place over the span of about two weeks and spoke with the employees about newcomers.

Unfortunately, the location was only bringing in about 6 or 7 new customers a week, which wasn't even enough to pay one employee for one day of work. I had to pass it up, because I felt that a tanning salon needed to bring in more people based on its location . . . flyers and newspaper ads weren't going to attract the multitudes!

Another business venture would've made me three to four times more profit during a fiscal year if I had been willing to sign on a mall lease that cost three times more than my strip mall location. The walk-by traffic was insanely higher in the mall, and I was selling an impulse-driven product. It's purely a numbers game. More people walking by and experiencing my product would've meant more people breaking out their wallets to buy. I opted for the location where lots of cars drove by and could easily see my store, and I lost an opportunity to earn a sizeable profit. Learn from my mistakes.

Moreover, if your business doesn't need a location with lots of walk-by traffic, don't waste your money on the lease. If you're paying for a retail pad, an office space, or a warehouse and it's not bringing in more revenues because you're there, that's money out of your pocket. My father always said that slicing a pie into more pieces doesn't mean you have more pie. Lower your overhead and don't lease out or buy property that isn't necessary or won't help your business perform any better.

Location Build-Out:

Go big or go home. One of the biggest mistakes start-up business owners make is the work-your-way-up-from-nothing mentality. Don't try to open up a taco shop with one table, two chairs, a microwave, and some tortillas. As with dating, first impressions are the most important in commerce. A half-baked business location could scare any would-be customers away, so start off right. There are ways to finance good ideas. I wouldn't buy a laptop from a guy in some obscure corner of a back alley strip mall that might not even be around for warranty issues when I can spend a little more at a well-established store that I know will be there when I need them.

Price Right:

Same goes for your pricing—too many entrepreneurs shoot themselves in the foot by trying to start out with bottom-dollar prices. The roofer says to himself, "I think I'll get my name out there by lowering my price, getting more jobs, gaining some experience, and showing that I do quality work." Before he knows it, he's getting calls from everybody in town, but guess what—not one person is willing to pay more than what his or her neighbor paid. He suddenly realizes that he worked so hard for pennies when he could've started off making as much as any other roofer on the same job.

Many businesses don't even offer coupons, because they don't like to instill that expectation of paying a lower price for a product that is worth more. The problem is that consumers just won't pay a premium price for something once they've experienced it for a discount. It's difficult to pay $950 for a cruise vacation ticket when you know that for that one week later in the year, you can probably find them for $500.

START MARKETING:

You'll learn soon enough that a fantastic business idea will generate zero profits if the public has no idea where you're at, what you're selling, and how great your deals are. From the day you start investing money into your business, you need to have a sizeable budget for marketing your idea. You can take advantage of several different advertising mediums, and for every business the different means of advertising have significantly different results. You'll need to track the efficacy of your advertising closely to discover which methods are most beneficial for your particular business.

Free Classifieds and Bulletin Boards. Learn to love what costs you nothing! You'll read about the classified ads over and over in this book, because I've seen phenomenal results from free advertising. You can't go wrong when you take advantage of the community's free marketing that is available to anybody. I place business ads several times a week on the free local Internet classified listings, and they generate ten times more traffic and income than my paid search-engine ads. Don't forget about the several bulletin boards at local businesses, college campuses, or public buildings.

Flyers. Many places will print up flyers for next to nothing. For $20–$50 you can usually get thousands of flyer ads that can be handed out or posted on doors and vehicles. Obviously, the nicer your flyers look, the better results you will see. Be aware that most people don't like strangers touching their cars and putting stuff in the door or windshield wipers that they have to take off and throw away. I wouldn't take this route unless I was really hurting for customers.

Coupon Mailers. There are several companies that send out coupon packs every month, and it's relatively inexpensive to include your own discount flyers for the bargain shopper to receive. Most people love to thumb through the stack of coupons and pick out the ones they might be interested in. The majority of unsolicited mail goes into the trash can unopened and unread, but these coupon books are almost always opened, which means your name will become familiar. I recently utilized this medium and sent out twenty thousand full-color, glossy, double-sided flyers for only $700. That's less than four cents for each home to know that I am in business and I have a great deal waiting for them. Send out more flyers, and your cost drops incrementally.

Valpak and Money Mailer are the two most popular coupon dealers you can work with, but if you shop around, there could possibly be a similar, more effective mailer business to advertise with in your community. They all have several statistics about how many people open their envelopes, average household income mapped out by areas, how big the average family is, what the age groups are, and so on.

Other coupon dealers will solicit you to provide discounts that they can publish on a card and sell to the public. It's free for you and can bring in lots of customers.

Niche Marketing Companies. It's overwhelming how many media marketing companies are out there pestering every business owner to advertise through them. There are newspapers, magazines, websites, event planners, and a whole conglomerate of multi-media marketers that will bug you day after day to market your business with them. Be smart about where you allocate your advertising dollars. Most of these businesses present bogus statistics that are sometimes misleading. Ask for discounts to do trial ads with them or call businesses that are currently marketing through them and ask what kind of results they've seen. You simply can't afford to waste your funds on media that won't produce results and get customers in your door.

Newspaper Ads. I know a loan officer who uses one single form of advertising. He pays for a ¼ front page color ad on the most popular classified ads in Utah, which is published every week and distributed all across several cities. Several thousand copies go out, and almost 100 percent of them get picked up by the public. His one small ad on the front of this paper generates more business for him than he can handle. If he figures out a way to take in more customers, I'm sure he'll find more ways to advertise his services.

Radio and TV. An effective way to advertise your business might be through radio and TV commercials. It's definitely the more expensive route, but if it produces results then there's the reason to pay for it. Be ready to spend some serious money, because TV and radio stations will want to schedule a lengthy time period of commercial spots to be aired day after day and week after week. Pricing varies depending on what time of the day you want your ad to air and on what station. After paying to have your commercial made with actors, voice professionals, photographers, or computer specialists, you could spend thousands of dollars before you even begin the marketing part. If done right, however, these commercials could pay off big!

Billboards. You can't help but see those big billboards while traveling down the highway. They are certainly a good option, as well. Again, every advertising medium isn't for every business, so don't tie up your funds in more expensive marketing tools unless you're fairly certain that they will produce results. Billboards are costly to hang a sign on. You usually enter a contract to lease the billboard for a certain number of months and then pay to have your sign designed and installed. Depending on the size and location, a billboard could cost from $500 to $10,000 per month.

One of my college Portuguese professors walked into class one day and shared with us the conversation he had just had with his son who is an attorney in Las Vegas. He said, "My son just called to let me know about the $300,000 bonus check he received this month . . . just a *bonus* check!" His son is an ambulance chaser and has a $50,000 monthly advertising budget that goes towards billboards.

Phone Books. Phone books provide a variety of advertising options. You can pay to have a simple, one inch listing in the yellow pages under a couple of different categories, or you can upgrade to a larger ad space with custom art and greater visibility. Some businesses pay to be on the outer cover (usually several thousand dollars per month) while others have an ad printed on the outer edges of the pages, which are visible when the book is closed. Still, other companies will glue refrigerator magnets to the outside of phone books or pay for an extra thick fold-out ad that protrudes from the middle of the book. Every home receives a copy of this phone book, so it's usually a good idea to make sure you are at least listed in the yellow pages.

Free, Free, Free. Again, free is what you're looking for, and oftentimes, you'll find your way into incredible advertising opportunities that won't cost you a dime. Call the local newspaper, and let them know you're open. If they come out and interview you in order to print an article about your product or services, you've hit the jackpot. Call the local TV shows that bring in guests to see if they'd be interested in having you on their show. Arrange to do giveaways with a favorite radio station that your target market probably listens to. The possibilities are only limited by your imagination.

Printed Gifts. Set up a table at the local mall and just give stuff away. Hand out T-shirts, pens, drinks, magnets, toys, or anything that might complement your business. Make sure that whatever you hand out has your information printed on it somewhere. People love free stuff, and if it's something they'll use over and over with your business name plastered all over it, they'll think of you when they're ready to buy.

Internet. Don't forget the power of the Internet. Of course, every business should have a web presence, so once you have your website up and running, submit it to all of the most popular search engines (Yahoo, Google, MSN, AOL, Shopzilla, Bizrate, and so on). This is discussed in the e-commerce chapter, but you should also be aware that there are several ways to market your business for free on the Internet. Email other related businesses and ask if you can post a link on their website that will bring traffic to yours. You can also set up affiliate programs where other websites actually sell your product for you and receive a small commission (5 to 10 percent) if somebody buys through them. Many information-rich sites are more than happy to direct their visitors to a good business.

Spread the Word. Now, the most effective means of advertising . . . *word of mouth.* If you truly have a great product or service, and people are happy with your business, they'll tell their friends. Nothing has more persuasive influence on an individual than friends or loved ones talking about your business and putting in a good word. It's also the most destructive means of advertising if your customers aren't happy with you. They say happy customers might tell four to seven friends about you, while disgruntled customers will vent and complain about you to fourteen of their friends. Maybe an incentive program that rewards your customers who send referrals your way could be the fuel-to-the-fire that your business needs.

Make Every Dollar Count. As a rule of thumb, you should be able to increase the amount of money you spend marketing your business and always see more revenues because of it. If you're spending $500 per month and grossing $15,000 in sales, you should be able to spend $1000 a month and generate $30,000 in sales. This doesn't necessarily need to be exact, but the point is to make sure you don't waste your precious money on ineffective advertising. Constantly track where your marketing funds are going and how many leads/sales each medium is bringing to your business. A good entrepreneur will rapidly learn the secrets to creating public recognition of his product. The sooner he learns how, when, and where to spend his marketing dollar, the sooner he will reap the benefits.

KEEP GOOD RECORDS:

It'll surprise you how much money will be going into and out of your bank account. Try not to forget that it's not all yours . . . especially the tithing portion. Every time you run a customer's credit card, accept their cash, or process a check to close a sale, you are accepting liability to pay an honest tax (just so you know, sales taxes are different in each state and vary according to products, and people who buy your product from out of state are generally exempt from paying a sales tax). Also, every time you spend money on things related to your business, you get a tax break. The best way to ensure that you are being honest in your taxes is to keep good records and hire a smart accountant. It's also the best way to avoid any heat from the IRS when they decide to audit you and your business.

Don't fool yourself into thinking that you can keep a mental record of all of your expenses and earnings. And even though most banking technology does a pretty good job of tracking your purchases and deposits, the details are frequently omitted, leaving you to wonder what you actually bought or sold that day. It's best to hang on to *all* of your receipts and organize your records at the end of each month. A filing cabinet along with individual folders for each month will come in handy. By keeping all of your expenses and sales on file, tax time will be so much easier for you and your accountant. The lingo for this is "keeping the books." Most people either procrastinate doing this until they create a mess that's beyond control, or they hire somebody to take care of the task. However you do it, keep records and know how your money is coming in and going out.

CUSTOMER SATISFACTION:

Many business owners swear up and down that customer happiness is the key to success. The philosophy is that if you bend over backwards for your customers, they'll be loyal for life and referrals will abound. Most entrepreneurs believe religiously in the mantra "the customer is always right."

I think it mostly depends on your particular type of business, but common sense would dictate that customer satisfaction *is* a must. Wal-Mart might be much more concerned about keeping a customer happy than Mr. Miller's Car Lot. Can you see why? What are the odds of Mr. Miller seeing a customer again within the next two to five years? Wal-Mart might see its customers on a daily basis (I know I shop there just about every day).

Unfortunately, the customer's-always-right attitude has gotten a little out of control, and many people abuse the policy. I witnessed somebody go to a store and buy some expensive exercise equipment to be used as a visual aid in a Sunday-school lesson . . . he never had any intention of keeping it. He got a full money refund a week later when he returned it. Would you want customers doing this to you and your business? I had a client ask me if he could return some furniture for an exchange or refund if his kids decided to pee on it. And he was dead serious! So, yes, treat your customers right, but don't let them take advantage of your kindness. Bigger stores can get away with their generous return policies, because they just send the returns right back to the supplier they bought it from and never lose a dime in the process.

Be prepared to back up your business and help out customers who really aren't getting what they paid for. If you ship them something that never arrives, you might have to eat the cost of shipping out another one. If they pay for something, make sure they get exactly what they expected. Leaving customers with busted or nonfunctional products or services is a bad, bad practice.

Not taking care of your customers could very easily come back to haunt you. The worst enemy out there for small business owners is a little thing known as a chargeback. An unsatisfied customer simply has to call her credit card company and claim that she didn't get what was paid for, and before you know it, the funds in your bank account completely disappear! You read that correctly—a credit card company has the authority to extract funds from your bank account after a transaction is completed and return them to the customer. You can fight it all you want, but it is almost always a losing battle. Fraudulent chargebacks are rampant today with people taking advantage of this process left and right, but hopefully, new laws will be issued to protect against it.

The biggest issue with customer satisfaction is your willingness to resolve any problems that arise, but other things will certainly factor into the level of happiness you instill in your clients. Just this week, I had a customer mention that they bought from me only because they thought I was friendly while my competitor wouldn't even take the time to say hi. I don't know if I'm extra friendly or my competitors are just brainless, but I've actually been told this on several occasions. Be genuinely kind and talkative with your customers, and they might just buy from you for the sole reason that they like you. A little charm can go a long way for the entrepreneur.

Trademarks, Copyrights, and Patents:

As you set up shop and see your business come to life, you will want to consider filing for trademarks, copyrights, or patents. Your name, logo, colors, and anything else that could be copied by your competitors who want to steal your customers should be protected in the early stages of development. The following section will help you understand exactly what each of these mean:

Copyright. "The legal right granted to an author, composer, playwright, publisher, or distributor to exclusive publication, production, sale, or distribution of a literary, musical, dramatic, or artistic work."[1]

Do not try to sell other people's stuff without their legal consent. You will be sued, and the cost or risk is not worth it. They can sue you for up to three times the damage, which means for every dollar of business that you steal from them, they can get that back from you times three. Usually, things that are copyrighted state that they are—websites, books, music, movies, and so forth. Most things that are copyrighted require that you pay the owner royalties if you'd like to market it.

Likewise, if you are going to build a business of something that is copyrightable, you better file for the copyright before somebody else does. There are people out there who look for other people's ideas just so they can copyright them as their own. Don't wait very long to do this.

Trademarks. Similar to copyrights are trademarks: "any name, symbol, figure, letter, word, or mark adopted and used by a manufacturer or merchant in order to designate his or her goods and to distinguish them from those manufactured or sold by others."[2]

Try to replicate somebody's logo, slogans, or name, and you can get sued. Most larger businesses have attorneys that attack as soon as trademark infringement occurs. You'll receive a cease and desist letter telling you to stop using their trademarked material immediately or face the legal consequences. Don't try to fight this battle. Again, when you come up with your own name, logo, and slogans, consider trademarking them before somebody else does.

Patent. "The exclusive right granted by a government to an inventor to manufacture, use, or sell an invention for a certain number of years."[3]

This is another legal technicality that you need to be careful with. If you want to sell a product (or process) that is patented, you must obtain permission from its owner. Sometimes a deal can be negotiated (with royalty fees) but most of the time it can't. If you have a widget that you've invented, file for a patent to prevent others from replicating your product/business and putting you out.

Patents have a lot of value. Many people buy up patent rights and sell them to others who are in the market for a business product. Others just invent something, file for a patent, and then sell the rights. If you have a successful business with a product protected by your patent, you have already built much more value into your business.

You have one year from the date of disclosing your product or process to the public to file for the patent if you would like to obtain exclusive rights. After that period, anybody can replicate your idea if it isn't patent-pending. Plan on spending upwards of $10,000 (in separate payments) and hiring an experienced lawyer to help you obtain a patent. The process can take a couple of years to finalize, but it's worth doing. A patent is good for seven years, and if you wish to renew your patent for another seven years, you can. After fourteen years, the product or process is free game for anybody to replicate. That's plenty of time to make your millions and claim your corner on the market.

Can you get around an existing patent? Yes . . . in most cases, the product or process must be at least 10 percent different (as mentioned before), but measuring this can be complicated. Make sure it's significantly different if you're entering into patented products or processes. Another thing to consider is that many patents are issued but do not stand up in court. This means that someone can receive a patent for something that neighbor Tom invented ten years ago. Neighbor Tom has been selling it and can prove that it was his idea first. They go to court and Tom can win, knocking down a patent that was issued.

Why spend the money on copyrights, patents, and trademarks? It prevents competition and preserves your business profile. Being lazy about filing for these could mean lost money to change your name and materials. Perhaps the most important reason to do these things—you cannot franchise a business unless this intellectual property is protected.

Say you do start opening franchises; Matthew Money likes your business and sees an opportunity for income so he pays a franchise fee to you and replicates your store as directed. He has all kinds of signs and product plastered with your name, logo, and slogan in his store with lots of money invested. Then, you get a nasty letter saying that somebody else has trademarked your name or whatever and that you have to immediately change everything that uses these things. It can happen!

Tip: do your research thoroughly before establishing certain aspects of your business. Don't flirt with danger—in other words, make sure you don't come too close to somebody else's protected names, products, processes, logos, slogans, and so on. Don't give other companies any excuse to take you to court. Larger companies will sue over the smallest little things. In many cases they just hope to sweat you out in court and make you go broke so that you'll close down shop.

Consider Franchising:

Another common term in the world of entrepreneurs is "turnkey." When big moneymakers get together and brag about their turnkey operations, they are saying that they have a business that earns money without them having to work. A turnkey business is like a well-oiled machine that just needs somebody to walk up and turn the key. Others refer to this as "passive income." Setting up a business that operates without you having to be present is a great goal to aim for.

Make your business as turnkey as possible by creating a system which produces enough income to finance the cost of operation and still have profits for your bank account. Otherwise, you've done nothing but created a job for yourself.

While working for yourself is preferable, it can have its disadvantages. Many entrepreneurs get caught up in the workings of the business- thinking that they are the only ones qualified to get the job done right. They begin to wear many hats and never delegate important tasks to employees that seem to not care as much about the business. The business grows and so does the workload, so the boss starts working sixty, seventy-five, and ninety hours a week to stay afloat. This is when they realize they have nothing more than a strenuous job and decide to quit. Knowing when to hire and how to train employees (management skills) will ultimately decide your success as an entrepreneur.

It is almost impossible to be completely detached from a business you own. You will certainly be involved emotionally and will probably need to dedicate some time to making sure it runs smoothly. Your manager might need time off for a newborn baby, or the holiday rush might require you to get your hands dirty, but the idea should be to free up as much time as possible in order to pursue other investments that will make you more money. Concentrate on setting up passive income systems and see how sweet life can be.

Once you have a business model that generates profits without the owner having to work, you open up a whole new means of making money. The world is full of investors—people looking to put their money in a place where it will multiply. If you can provide an opportunity for people to buy a business that will earn them money without having to work, they will pay you well for it. Franchising is a wonderful way to make some serious money, but you must have a very efficient system that earns impressive profits without having to be owner-operated.

Usually a franchise agreement simply means that somebody is buying your business model from you. History shows that buying a franchise is much safer than trying to start up your own venture, because you're buying into a proven system that is already successful. They pay you a lump sum of money to give them the knowledge and assistance required to open up a functional business. Franchise agreements almost always include a small percentage to be paid in royalties. If you are selling two franchises a year for $25,000 each with agreements to receive 8% royalty fees from each location, you're suddenly earning way more money without having to work for it. Yes, as corporate management, you will need to regulate and oversee the different branches, but the additional workload is minimal compared to what you earn from each franchise that is opened.

When and if you get to this point, pat yourself on the back and know that you have done something that few people have the ability to do. Then go arrange for an attorney to write up your franchise agreement, and start marketing your business like there's no tomorrow.

Go and Do:

In conclusion, these are some simple and fundamental steps you will need to take if you wish to start your own business. It's certainly not an easy task and requires creativity, ambition, and the willingness to take action. There are many other issues that a business owner deals with such as unemployment, liability insurance, worker's compensation, utilities, and so on. Plenty of books have been written on the subject (available at the library) that can walk you through the entire process with some of the most boring details you'll ever read in your life. They are important, however, and are worth knowing if they can keep you from running a business illegally.

No matter what your plans are—job or not—it's a great experience to start up your own business. I highly recommend giving it a try. Success doesn't always come the first time around, so believe in yourself and constantly brainstorm for potential business ideas. Your next idea, if executed properly, could be worth millions of dollars.

Exercise:

Over the next month, concentrate on identifying at least two business ideas that could possibly be successful. Develop the two ideas by considering each of the steps listed in this chapter and how you would do each one. Take the time to learn how to do every single step for your business ideas. And, if you're on to something promising, why not go for it?

Notes

1. Answers.com, "Copyright," http://www.answers.com/copyright.
2. Dictionary.com, "Trademark," http://www.dictionary.com/browse/trademark.
3. Dictionary.com, "Patent," http://www.dictionary.com/browse/patent.

9

Become a Salesman

Just as you learned to become an effective gospel teacher, it's important to acquire sales skills if you wish to be successful. Yes, you can become an Internet marketing hermit who never has to speak to a soul, but being able to apply certain salesmanship techniques will be necessary in all walks of life. Even if you hate the sales environment, it will be worth putting yourself in a sales pitch situation enough to develop a knack for it.

Knocking Doors to Sell the Gospel

Think back to the first time you had to knock doors and speak to people cold turkey about converting to the true gospel of Jesus Christ. Was that not one of the hardest things you ever had to do? It's not easy getting into a door when you're bringing somebody a whole new outlook on God and religion. The funny part about it is that the most precious thing in the world is 100 percent free, but the best salesman ever couldn't close this deal with most people.

I remember companions who would completely freeze up when it came to knocking doors and contacting in the streets. They would either refuse to talk or go through the textbook, robotic routine of smiling, shaking hands, and introducing themselves as a missionary and then would have nothing else to say. I worked with a companion who for three months straight would smile, say who he was, and pause awkwardly until somebody else took over, because he was too nervous to say anything else.

My brother had a companion who completely collapsed the first time he gave an introduction when they knocked a door. His knees buckled and he fell over sideways on the guy's porch. They didn't get in that time, but the fellow invited my brother and his companion to come back when they hadn't had as much to drink beforehand.

Selling the gospel was a little bit different from trying to sell some random product. In reality, it was the toughest and most complicated sale a person would ever have to close, but because we knew it was so important, we did it with passion and zeal, making it uplifting and fun. We all knew that the nature of our calling was to preach repentance and baptism (trying to sell a nifty cleaning mop doesn't muster up as much conviction). It was easy under these circumstances to give people a little push in the right direction. If we couldn't convince our investigators to come unto Christ by keeping his commandments and entering into covenants with him, it was almost a waste of time.

Pushing and Nudging

I know that there were several seeds planted when people wouldn't accept what we had to offer, but there was no gray area in between as far as I was concerned. If we weren't there doing our best to commit investigators to convert and be baptized, we were not fulfilling our calling. The missionaries who feared inviting people undoubtedly had much less success than the missionaries who were bold enough to invite during the first discussion and repeatedly throughout the teachings.

Do investigators have to know that the Church is true to be baptized? Yes. But do they have to know the Church is true to accept the baptismal invitation? Of course not! I thought I had to teach people all of the discussions and hear them say they had read the Book of Mormon, prayed about Joseph Smith, and knew the Church was true before I even hinted at baptism. Boy, was I wrong! Four or five months later when I figured out a little more about my role as a missionary, I became a little bolder and saw spectacular results because of it. I carry a conviction in my heart that all people urgently need to hear the message of the Restoration and be baptized by the proper authority, and I was willing to push my way into homes from time to time as a means of getting the people of Peru to listen.

One afternoon, after knocking several doors with no luck, we came across a man who was just returning home as we knocked on his neighbor's door. He fumbled through his keys frantically to get inside before we could approach him. Lucky for him, we were fast on our feet. As we introduced ourselves and tried our best to open the conversation to religion, he expressed that he really wasn't interested.

I had wasted too much time getting turned down by one person after another and was tired of it, so I decided to take a different approach. I don't recommend this, but sometimes you gotta do what you gotta do. I asked him if he truly believed in God, to which he replied that he did. I told him that if he really did believe in God then he should take a few minutes to learn something about him. I made it clear that we traveled from a distant part of the world to bring a special message about God and that he was about to pass up an opportunity that might only come once in a lifetime. Interestingly, he changed his mind after the little guilt trip I gave him and invited us to come in for a brief message. About two months later, he and his family were baptized and ordained members of the church—all because of a small push to get in his door.

Learning the right buttons to push by word choice and timing could transform you into a master salesman. A successful salesman has so much the advantage in this world. I know individuals who would spend their summers working in sales for pest control, security systems, or satellite TV and would earn more money in three months than many will in a whole lifetime. Very few are all that successful at this, so I don't recommend spending your summers as a sales rep for a similar product unless you know you have a gift for sales (believe me, you will be approached by recruiters over and over). Learning the techniques of salesmanship is, without a doubt, a stepping stone towards abundant wealth.

Confidence Is Key

I'll be the first to testify that the Spirit is the greatest missionary known to mankind and that we are mere instruments in the hands of God. I also know from scripture that an essential attribute when acting as one of these instruments is *confidence,* which we are endowed with when worthy. Doctrine and Covenants 121:45 says "Let thy bowels also be full of charity towards all men, and to the household of faith, and let virtue garnish thy thoughts unceasingly; then shall thy confidence wax strong in the presence of God; and the doctrine of the priesthood shall distil upon thy soul as the dews from heaven."

Confidence can make or break a deal. Being bold, but not overbearing, was so important in missionary work, and it's just as important when it comes to product sales. Sadly, there are sales floors full of phone operators that will do anything to make a commission. Many of these sales floors are patrolled by cops due to the fact that the salesmen will snort cocaine and do whatever they can to get high . . . because when they're high, they're confident. This is silly!

Strengthen Your Self-Esteem

Confidence can be obtained by so many other, more permanent means. Work out, dress nice, seek out education, surround yourself by people who are positive and motivational, and above all—be worthy of the Spirit. Just know that if you're doing your best to convince somebody to open up his pocketbook and give you money, you need to radiate confidence. If low self-esteem is an issue, work on overcoming that. You're not in high-school anymore, and you can live with fewer inhibitions.

A Few Communication Pointers:

Confidence is reflected by eye contact, body language, tone of speech, smiling, knowledge, and several other factors.

- Looking somebody in the eyes communicates honesty whereas looking away or at the ground can appear shady and cause mistrust.
- Folding your arms communicates that you are closed off and unapproachable.
- Mumbling and stuttering makes it hard for people to pay attention to your pitch.
- Not smiling tells them you're serious, so lighten things up a little and make the conversation enjoyable. Even if you're on the phone, smile, because they will hear your smile in the way you speak.
- Know what you're talking about. Product knowledge is one of the most important sales attributes I look for when shopping. If I come across somebody who knows their stuff, I listen, and I'm ten times more likely to buy from them than the guy that has little to say.
- Be happy . . . even when you're not. That "fake it 'til you make it" attitude is one you'll want to adopt.

Missionary Skills = Sales Skills

You acquired many salesmanship tactics as a missionary whether you know it or not. I recommend locating a copy of *The Closers* by Ben Gay III and reading through it. You will be stunned at how similar it is to the *Preach My Gospel* manual. We can discuss a few more sales principles in this chapter, but I believe you will best learn by reading a book focused on the subject and then studying the many salesmen you will encounter when you're out shopping. It is a wise investment . . . even if you never go into a sales-oriented profession.

Things to Pay Attention To

Word Choice

Surprise, surprise—the words and expressions you use throughout a sales pitch can have an enormous psychological effect on a customer. Some great salesmen are able to relieve the tension a little with phrases like, "I know you're thinking I'm a salesman, and it's my job to sell you this product, right? Well, I don't want to sell you anything. Let me just explain to you why other people have bought this product, and if you like what you hear, you're more than welcome to give it a try. If it doesn't fit into your budget or it just won't work for you and your family, don't buy it. Does that work for you?"

Simple phrases like "give it a try" are just euphemisms for "buy it," but when a salesman makes the decision to sound a little non-committal, people are more likely to feel less guilty about spending their money. Other phrases such as "pencil it in" work very well on purchase contracts. Any terminology that somewhat softens the blow and doesn't make it sound like they're stuck with something can do wonders for a salesman.

The best way to learn the psychology of a sales presentation and what word choice suits you and your personality is by studying and memorizing scripts. There are numerous books on the subject with word-for-word sales pitch scenarios. Verbally practicing what other successful salesmen have said is a fantastic way to become a deal closer yourself.

Talking to the Right Person

One thing to keep in mind when trying to sell somebody a product is whether or not you are talking to the decision maker. People will do anything they can to avoid salesmen and pressure tactics that are so commonly misused. The decision maker might hide out in the car while she sends her husband in to gather a little information that will help her decide to purchase or not. If you figure out that you aren't speaking to the decision maker, don't waste your breath until you can get that person in front of you. Usually you can plan in advance with appointments and invite both husband and wife. When I'm selling anything that costs over a couple hundred dollars, I ask the person if the spouse is going to make it to the appointment. If the spouse cannot, I try to reschedule at a time when both can be present.

Just so you know, it's usually the wife that wears the pants and ultimately decides whether or not to purchase. If she doesn't want her hubby to buy something, he's normally smart enough not to splurge. Speak to the wife as much as you do the husband . . . or even more. You could probably speak solely to the wife and only help your chances of closing a deal, but be considerate and direct the conversation to both.

Analyze and Adapt

Just like you couldn't really teach a missionary lesson unless you talked to a person and discovered their needs, it is difficult to sell a product unless you pay close attention to the customer. You must constantly adapt the pitch to the personality of the customer. This doesn't necessarily mean that you need to harmonize with every personality type on this planet and be everybody's best friend (although that would help). It just means that you should listen and analyze at all times in order to adapt your sales presentation to the customer. Focus on how the product will benefit them instead of just the features. Features are great, but people are sold when they see and believe that a product will benefit them. In short, listen, adapt, and focus on *benefits* rather than features.

Positive Response Questions

A neat technique that is employed by any salesman who knows what he's doing is the positive response technique. Every time you can get a "yes" out of a customer's mouth, you are that much closer to getting a "yes" when you ask for the close. Repeatedly asking questions that are sure to get a positive response is the primary focus in this sales strategy. "This is a good looking car, isn't it?" "Wouldn't you love to relax in a hot tub that has over twenty massage jets just for your back?" "You could have some fun with this thing, couldn't you?" Obviously, you can overdo it if you aren't careful. Keep a good balance in the conversation by allowing the customer to give positive input every once in a while, but don't repeat questions like those above unless you want to kill the deal. Common sense will dictate the situation.

Ask for the Close

There is no certain time to close a deal. With some people, the right time might come at the very beginning of the conversation. Other times you will close a deal midway through your pitch. There is no textbook instruction on this part of salesmanship. You have to simply pay attention and take advantage of the opportunity when it presents itself. You must, however, have the courage to ask for the close. Many customers want you to ask them to buy. Often times a salesman will go through his whole sales pitch and have the customers sold from the very beginning, but he'll avoid asking for the close . . . thus, kissing his commission goodbye. A basic "What do ya say? Let's give it a try!" will work wonders for any salesman.

I admit that to this day, being in a situation where I'm consciously trying to push a decision onto somebody is uncomfortable, and I prefer to avoid it. Wanna know why sales positions pay so well? Go fill out an application and try telemarketing for a week. I wouldn't wish a job of making outbound cold-calls on anybody, but some people are okay with it and make a fantastic living off of pressure sales. Being a salesman can get complicated, but it doesn't necessarily have to feel so uncomfortable if you go about it correctly.

Believe in Your Product

By believing in a product and developing an attitude that you are helping the customer in the deal . . . that the money they are spending is worth equal to or less than what they are receiving, you will close deals more often. If the product you're trying to sell isn't worth the price tag on it, maybe you shouldn't be trying to sell it. A good deal should be mutually beneficial, and if you know that it is, you will be much more persuasive in your sales presentation.

When you believe in the product, you promote it with passion. The worst attribute you could possess is apathy when it comes to sales (or anything for that matter). Apathy comes from the Greek word *apathos,* where *a* means without and *pathos* means passion. When you are excited about something and really feel that the customer is benefiting from the deal you are presenting, they will be excited about it also. Passion and excitement are contagious. As Enoch preached like "a wild man" and converted a whole city to the gospel, your enthusiasm will ensure your success as a closer (Moses 6:38).

The list goes on and on, so a good idea would be to study books about salesmanship and analyze all of the salesmen you come across from here on out. Pay attention to the techniques they use and whether you feel that it encouraged the sale or made you want to run for cover.

You Can Sell Anything

There is not a product in this world more difficult to sell than the gospel. If you could convince people to change their lives, pay tithing, make temple covenants, and accept church callings, you have the potential to sell ice cubes to Eskimos. Throughout life, be confident, believe in your product, study salesmanship, and practice applying sales techniques that you need to develop.

You will need to be conscious about your sales techniques each time you are giving a pitch. It requires hundreds and hundreds of experiences to develop true salesmanship talent, but anybody can do it. When you can work magic and get the most hard-nosed, tight-wad shoppers to open their checkbooks and give you their money, you know that you've accomplished something. There's a strange joy that comes from sales when you can see your skills developing and more deals closing. The power to influence people will greatly affect the level of abundance you obtain over the next several years.

Exercises:

In your saving exercise of chapter 14 where you will flip a bargain product that you find, focus on actually giving a sales pitch over the phone and in person. Try to measure your methods of communication with your customers. Do they feel like you're trying to sell them on it, or did they feel like you were just helping them know more about the product? Were they appreciative or did they close up and find an excuse to leave without buying? Sales books will help you respond to any excuse imaginable that people use not to buy.

10

E-commerce for Greeny RMs

It's no big secret that the Internet has opened up a glorious new dimension to wealth-building systems. What seems like eons ago, everything to do with business transactions was done in person, over the phone, or through snail mail. Now you can shop for anything from anywhere at anytime because of amazing advancements in computer technology and the conception of the Internet. This incredible invention has made it possible for millions of entrepreneurs like you and me to join the ranks of the rich.

Let's take a look at a few examples. Just recently a couple of guys decided to take advantage of webcam technology and create a website where users could share videos with the world for free. You've probably heard of YouTube.com before. Sounds like a pretty simple concept, wouldn't you say? A website where you can post your own videos for free and then view all the videos that the rest of the world has posted.

It was such a great idea that what might just be the world's most famous website of all time, Google search engine, bought out YouTube for a small sum of 1.65 billion dollars! While the idea for YouTube is very basic, the media power it generates is astounding. In the year 2006 this Internet hotspot generated a daily average of 65,000 new videos uploaded and over 100 million videos viewed each and every day.

Another pinnacle of genius was reached in 1995 when a broken laser pointer was sold on an online auction for $14.83. Yes, eBay was born and the world will never be the same. Within three years, this online business went public, and its founders became instant billionaires. This one Internet concept has been the means for thousands upon thousands of people becoming self-employed millionaires.

EBay now owns PayPal, which is an online banking website that processes payments for other Internet businesses and generates billions in revenue itself. The vast majority of all online transactions are processed by PayPal, which means PayPal is earning 3 to 4 percent of every dollar spent. My websites receive credit card payments through PayPal and it costs me right around 3 percent of every order processed.

More Realistic Examples

So we've seen a few dreamlike Internet concepts that have generated billions in revenue, but let's take a look at a couple of down-to-earth examples that could very easily be you in the near future. One returned missionary who I know very well was looking around for his eternal companion as he worked on his college education. He found a girl who unfortunately remained his girlfriend for the next five years before they reached an official breakup.

The funny thing is that having such a relationship gave this guy plenty of time to fiddle around with other things. While earning his college degree, he focused on web design and started playing around on the computer a little. He actually started off by buying a package deal of some paintball gear on eBay. He took the parts of the package that he didn't need and posted them back on eBay, which he sold for way more than what he paid for the whole bundle the week before. You can say that he caught the fever! He soon researched a few suppliers and manufacturers, set up his own website, and began making some serious cash.

Now, this guy runs an eBay store and two other paintball websites that generate tens of thousands of hits (visitors) each week. He drop-ships the majority of his orders, which means he never even sees the products. The manufacturer just ships them out for him. He travels whenever he wants and easily turns his vacations into "business trips" for tax purposes.

He happens to still be single, so late nights out and sleeping in are no problem for this bachelor. He works when he chooses and plays ten times more than just about anybody out there working for the same salary. I can't say exactly how much money his online business generates, but I know for a fact that he could pay for a very fancy home in cash and have plenty left over to keep living a nice life. Do you know a twenty-eight-year-old who has enough money in the bank to buy a house with cash and has absolutely no debt to his name? If you do, pay attention to what he's doing and see to it that you follow suit. Better than that, pay attention to this chapter and create an online business like this guy did.

Another close friend has a couple of websites that he uses to generate some extra income on the side. He hired several students, teacher's aides, and professors to write up compilations of class notes and summaries that would give somebody all the information necessary to pass certain college classes. He paid to have a professional website built that would market his class notes and sells them to college students all over the United States. They pay him a reasonable sum of money and in turn download the electronic file from his website so they can pass their classes (that they probably never attend).

This friend also set up an affiliate credit card referral website, which sends prospective borrowers to fill out credit card applications with the company that can best serve them. For each person who clicks on a link in his website and fills out an application, he earns anywhere from $60 to $160 and does absolutely nothing in the process. Passive income opportunities like this are everywhere, but will you take the time to brainstorm for ideas and actually build a website to implement them?

A Website Is an All-the-Time Employee that Requires Little Pay

I have a website for my furniture business, which accounts for about 30 percent of my gross sales. It took me a couple of weeks to set it up during my spare time, but now it is a 24/7 money-generating system that requires little to no attention from me.

I go to sleep at night and my Internet store stays open for anybody in the world to buy my product. I post all the information necessary for a customer who is shopping to understand my business and what they are buying, and nearly every day I wake up with more money in my bank account than I had when I jumped in bed. It requires no sales pitches or lengthy customer chatting to seal the deal, which means I don't have to be a people person or a salesman. Doesn't that sound ideal? It costs me thousands of dollars each month to operate my retail storefront location, but my Internet store runs itself for a whopping $20 per month!

Benefits of Running an Internet Business:

1) 24/7 operations, which means income when sleeping or vacationing

2) Worldwide market
3) Easy to generate traffic
4) You can do background management on whatever schedule you fancy
5) Fewer or even no employees
6) No experience necessary
7) Easy setup and maintenance
8) Less customer service needs to be provided as most can be automated
9) Drop-shipping is much easier
10) Low overhead and advertising costs
11) Unlimited potential for wealth
12) No dress code . . . my favorite

How to Begin

We know that there is an unlimited potential for wealth when it comes to e-commerce, but the question is "How do I get started?" It's easier than you ever imagined. You need to know nothing about web design or complex computer languages to set up and operate a successful, profit-generating Internet business. You can either learn all of the complicated behind the scene coding that websites are made up of, or you can find programs that allow you to automatically set up web pages and configure their functions with the click of a button.

I recommend starting out with these basic do-it-yourself web design programs, and then later on, you can figure out the more complicated stuff if you wish. The first step would be finding one of these automated programs that is easy to use and affordable. If you visit www.universaltrainingcenter.com and click on the e-commerce link, you will find a way to download one of these programs. You can try it free for a month and decide whether it works for you. If not, there are other automated programs available, but this is the most affordable and the easiest to use for most people.

Your website doesn't have to be perfect before launching it on the Internet. Ask for feedback from visitors, and let your friends and family pitch in ideas that will help you get a fully functional and sharp looking website. Due to certain limitations on these automated web design programs, you will probably want to invest a little money and have a professional designer build you a top-notch website after a while. When you are ready to have a professional design, visit www.elance.com and post your project so that designers can bid and compete for your job (web specialists from all over the world can build your site for much less than you might pay locally). But you'll definitely want to build your own as you get started so that you can manage it and make it look somewhat like you want it to.

Choose a Domain

The very first step in setting up a website is, of course, the domain name. Visit www.godaddy.com, and you can type in your ideas to see if the domain is available or already owned. This website can also give you additional ideas that are related to the words that you type in, which is very helpful.

More than likely, you will actually name your business based on what domains are available that match your name ideas. For example: You want to call your new luxury diaper bag company Poop Purse, but you find that www.pooppurse.com is already owned by somebody else. It's not a good idea to name your company one thing and then have a totally different domain name. Make sure your name is easy to remember, easy to spell, and communicates clearly what your business is all about.

You might even want to reserve domains that are spelled similarly to the one you will use. I purchased three different domains for one website—www.monstersak.com, www.monstersac.com, and www.monstersack.com.

Set Up a Shopping Cart (Payment Processing)

As you build your website, you will need to set up a payment method for customers to securely purchase whatever it is you're selling. This is referred to as the "shopping cart" program in e-commerce lingo. The automated web design program I direct you to in this book is integrated with PayPal (a big plus considering that all Internet shoppers can trust PayPal). You only need to set up a PayPal merchant account, and you will find instructions on how to link it with your website.

If you prefer to process your payment through other banks, there are ways to do it, but you will need to know a little more about web design to make it happen. You will have to purchase a shopping cart program and configure it into your website. Seek help if you feel inclined to do this.

Business Ideas

We won't really discuss possible business ideas in this chapter. The purpose is to focus on how to set up an e-commerce system. I will assume that you can use your own creativity to find something that fits your interests and ambitions. Obviously, you will need a tangible business idea before delving into the website stage, so start thinking.

Publish and Advertise

Once you have your business idea solidified, you've downloaded an automated web design program, and you've secured your domain, it will be time to ensure that the world can find you online. There are several ways to advertise online. Some are free and most are relatively inexpensive. My favorite methods are affiliate websites, search engines, and free classified ads.

An affiliate website is one that attracts people who would be interested in your product. Usually, you can arrange a deal with another business owner to do some mutual advertising for each other. If he sells couches and you sell something related, like beds, you could probably help each other out by putting a link on your websites in case people shopping for beds are also looking for couches and vice versa. This might not be the number one, most effective way to find shoppers, but every little bit helps. Affiliate programs are definitely an option to consider. As mentioned previously, you can even sell your product through other people's websites.

Search engines such as Google, Yahoo, MSN, Shopzilla, and so forth are an incredible way to attract people to your website. Each engine online has a set of instructions on how to submit your website and have it show up on their listings.

Hopefully, you already know how a search engine works. People type in a word in a search engine and instantaneously a list of websites related to that word pops up on the screen. Two types of listings appear with each keyword search—the naturalistic (organic) listings and the paid advertisement listings. You will want your website to be in both, but you will appear only in the paid advertising listings for the first little while.

The naturalistic listings are completely free and show up in an order determined by a complex calculation that the search engine uses. Probably the most important factor in determining the order that the links are displayed in is the number of visitors a website has received. If you attract a lot of people to your website, the search engine will recognize that you're the most popular one related to a keyword on your page, and it places a link to your website higher in the order. Many complicated steps can be taken to improve your website quality and boost your position in the naturalistic listings (this is called "search engine optimization"), but you will need the help of a professional to accomplish this.

The easy way to appear in the top listings of search engine results is to pay for ad words. You basically bid on a word saying how much you will pay to have a person click on your link when he types in a certain word on a search engine. Example: I sell an exotic breed of Bengal kittens and will pay 50 cents to have Google send a shopper to my website when they type in the word Bengal. If somebody else is in the same business and is willing to pay 75 cents for every click, they appear higher than me in the list.

In these search engines, you decide on how much you are willing to pay for clicks on each different word related to your website, and you also establish a daily and monthly budget so that you don't go broke. My daily limit on one website is $30, which gets me about forty-five to fifty visitors each day who are looking specifically for my product. Google is the most popular search engine, so visit www.adwords.google.com to set up your pay-per-click advertising.

Some people are so effective at this keyword advertising that they generate sales revenues much higher than what they spend on search engine advertising. I recently spoke with an entrepreneur who claimed that for every $100 he spends on keyword advertising, he generates $10,000 in business. Keep that in mind when you start spending your advertising money.

But say that paying to have search engines send shoppers your way isn't working so well. Fortunately, there are amazing, free classified ads in virtually every region of the world. In my present area, I know of four major classified ads that generate tens of thousands of visitors each and every day. For the outrageous cost of $0, I post ads on these classifieds a couple of times a week. Some of them have counters and show exactly how many people click on your ad to look at it. From just one of these free online classified ads, I get over three times as many hits from shoppers who are looking for my specific product than I do from the best search engines on the web. You can't beat free!

One really good, worldwide classifieds website is www.craigslist.org. Take a look at it and find the region nearest to your home—I guarantee you that thousands of people in your vicinity who want to find a good deal are looking through those ads every day.

Usually the local news stations will have a really nice website that includes a free classifieds section where you can post anything you want. Take advantage of these, and get people to visit your website. It's a simple fact that the more people you can get to look at what you're selling, the more product you will sell.

You Know, Now Go!

That's really all you need to know about e-commerce in order to get started. Pretty simple, wouldn't you say? Form a business idea, select a domain, download an automated web design program, build and publish your website, include a shopping cart, start advertising, and watch the money pour into your account.

Keep in mind that a website can be used to sell products (that you store or have drop-shipped by the manufacturer), information (such as how to get rich quick), services (like brick laying), computer programs (like accounting calculators), or even advertising (with banners and links to other websites). There are innumerable ways to make money online, and once you get started, you might find it so easy that you end up with five or six different websites generating income for you while all you do is click a few buttons every week. Regardless of your goals and aspirations in life, you will need a website one day, so you might as well get started.

Exercise:

Put down this book and go to www.universaltrainingcenter.com to download the website designer program on your computer. Set up the free trial version and build your own personal website with information about yourself, pictures, and miscellaneous features. Be sure to explore and experiment with all of the options such as video files, music files, bouncing letters, spinning pictures, fading text, and so on.

Within the next thirty days, have a business idea that you can experiment with and build a commercial website. It doesn't matter if you plan on seriously developing the business idea; the point is to understand the process fully and obtain some experience that will benefit you when you find your million-dollar idea.

11

Paying Taxes Wisely

By learning to pay your taxes carefully and strategically, you will save yourself more money than you might imagine. A person who learns the ins and outs of the tax system could easily finish up 30 percent wealthier than the ignoramus who never invests the time or energy to learn anything about it.

Know Tax Laws

Yes, you can and should hire an accountant who is experienced and full of legal counsel who will help you pay less in taxes, but studying books that help you understand the loopholes and tax breaks available to you is a must. It is your responsibility to know what deductions you can apply to your reported income, so don't plan on relying solely on your accountant's knowledge. It is also important to be as honest a tax payer as you are a tithe payer . . . which better be 100 percent integral.

Are you rolling in money at this point in your life? Probably not, but if you're paying attention to the things you are reading in this book, it won't be long before you're earning a considerable amount of income. You'll need to understand the way taxes work and know how to avoid paying what you don't really have to. Start learning now what you might not necessarily need to apply for another year or two, and you will be much better prepared to save yourself thousands of dollars.

Tax Breaks Are Not Unethical

You can take several steps to ensure you pay Uncle Sam the least amount of your hard-earned money. Some claim that they want to pay more in taxes in order to give back to their country while others preach that taking advantage of all of the available tax breaks is an unethical practice. Let me start by explaining this: we live in a country that has a very, very complicated tax system. Try filling out your own tax forms if you don't believe me. The smartest people I know wouldn't understand the language the government uses on 99 percent of the necessary forms. Although the system is complex, it is designed to give deductions and breaks to those who dig for them.

A man should do everything he can to take advantage of the myriad tax laws and pay the least amount possible when April 15 arrives. It is ludicrous to believe that applying every tax break you are entitled to is a wrongful practice. Taking advantage of the tax codes and making sure that you don't pay one cent more than you have to could eventually make the difference between broke or loaded.

According to Diane Kennedy and Garrett Sutton in their book *Real Estate Loopholes*, "There are over 500,000 pages of written tax law. And, what's more, it is constantly changing and being modified. Every day is a new day when it comes to taxes! Consider that there were over 400 IRS Code changes for 2001. For every Code change, there are one to five Treasury Regulations, Revenue Rulings, Revenue Procedures, and eventually multiple Tax Court cases. Over 400 Code changes occurred in 2001, which was considered pretty uneventful when it came to tax changes."[1]

Pay Up

First thing's first—do pay your taxes. We live in an amazing country with freedoms, privileges, and luxuries that most people in this world can only dream about. Being able to drive down a nicely paved highway with law enforcement agencies protecting your rights is worth paying taxes for . . . not to mention the schools, parks, and welfare programs.

Trying to evade the taxes that you owe is nothing short of stupidity. You might not get caught the first time, but it will catch up to you eventually, and you may just find yourself spending some quality time in a jail cell. Death and taxes! Two things you can always count on. There's no getting around it, so learn how to do it right from the beginning . . . and then make sure you pay your dues. This requires a well-planned budget that puts back a percentage each month of what you will owe the government that year.

Read a Simplified Tax Booklet

Once again, I suggest you pick up an educational book on the subject. This chapter will just skim the surface of a few examples that could benefit you in the nearby future. There are tax books written for small business owners, for real estate investors, for corporations, and so on. Forget about trying to read them all. Unless you have a boring life with nothing better to do, it's not wise to learn every loophole applying to every income scenario.

Choose a general tax topic that applies to you and your situation, and study it through. Keep a copy close by and highlight the information you believe might save you a buck. Review it before meeting with your accountant, and make sure you buy the latest editions each year as the tax laws are constantly changing.

Accountants Are Worth Their Hire

Definitely be selective when choosing an accountant that you will work with. They don't charge very much ($200–$1000) compared to the kind of money they will save you. You could very easily pay your taxes with the help of one accountant and then bring your records to another accountant a month later, and she will show you how she could've saved you $10,000. I hear these "if only" stories quite often from businessmen that finally find the right accountant. A good accountant will know how to structure your earnings in a way that requires you to pay much less to the government.

Asking around is usually the best way to locate an experienced professional. Talk to business owners, and find out what they think about their accountant. Hopefully, you will know enough about taxes from your leisure reading to determine whether an accountant will help you or hurt you. If you think you know enough to skip an accountant and file your taxes yourself, chances are you're mistaken. It's good to be independent, but it could cost you way more money than it's worth.

Tax Tips

The following insights are not intended to be legal or tax advice. Please speak with your accountant for more up-to-date and detailed explanations of how to apply these tax breaks to your situation. The following list is only provided to inform you about different possibilities.

Self-Employed

Running your own business requires expenses that most people don't come across as an employee. An intelligent entrepreneur will realize that almost all activity can be directly related to his work and counted as an expense . . . even vacations! If you happen to have a home office, vehicle expenses such as maintenance, mileage, or loan interest can be discounted from your gross profits. Equipment, labor, supplies, inventory, rent, and many other things can be deducted or depreciated from your revenues.

The government wants to help you be successful, which encourages a strong and thriving economy. With a little research, you can discover the various deduction possibilities so you can benefit from the tax breaks designed especially for business owners.

Real Estate Investments

Another way the government encourages a strong economy is through tax breaks given to home owners and investors. This is one reason why renting is just crazy. The interest you pay on your loan along with maintenance and improvements are things that are deducted from your net income. For example: You might earn $30,000 in a year and pay out $10,000 in rent. If you own your own home and earn the same $30,000, but you have paid $10,000 in interest and maintenance for your house, you'll only be taxed on $20,000 as opposed to the full $30,000 when you rent. Plug numbers and you'll see the true cost of ownership is much less if you're not taxed on such a large portion of your income. Maybe the net cost of living is lowered to around $7,000 when you consider the tax advantages. Again, this is just a hypothetical example to give an idea . . . true calculations will be somewhat different depending on your tax brackets. As tax laws change every year, this chapter could very well be outdated by the time you read it.

Depreciation is also factored in and lowers the amount of taxes you will owe at the end of the year. Depreciation is the opposite of appreciation. Although the real estate market consistently appreciates and equity builds, the government says that a property actually loses value as it ages. This is great for you, because you can calculate it out as a loss, which means you didn't earn as much money on paper and you won't have to pay as much in taxes.

Another break for home owners is a rule stating that if you occupy a property for two out of the first five years that you own it, you don't have to pay taxes *period* when you sell it. The law allows up to $500,000 for a couple or $250,000 per individual in capital gains to go into your bank account tax free. This is a huge blessing, and I encourage you to plan your investments in a way that will allow you to take advantage of this break.

Some tax laws also allow you to roll your equity into a "like property" within six months of selling an investment and defer any taxes from the capital gains. This is called a 1031 exchange, and you will probably need to understand it one day.

Many tax laws are associated with real estate, and by becoming familiar with the ones that apply to your specific properties, you can avoid paying too much in taxes.

Income

You pay for many things on a day-to-day basis that can be counted as a necessary expense on your tax forms. The more deductions you are aware of, the less income you can show when filing, which means you owe less money to the government. Some deductions include medical bills, tuition, loan interest, and a whole bunch of other things. Again, find a tax booklet that can coach you through some of these deductions and know what you can legally calculate out of your net income figure.

Documentation

Above all, keep good records and hang on to your receipts. It is critical that you are diligent in your record keeping, because every receipt you throw away could be worth money. If you trash a receipt for something that cost you $10.00 and you find yourself paying 20 percent taxes, that little piece of paper might have saved you a buck or two!

No matter how smart you are, you aren't a computer that can recall every penny you spent over the span of a year. Buy a little filing drawer and label a folder for each month of the year. At least once a month, update your folders by inserting all of the receipts you have and calculating where your money was spent and why. By accurately maintaining your records, you will be able to spend less time doing your taxes, and you will have proof in case the IRS decides to audit you and test your honesty.

Exercise:

- Find a tax guide at your local library (don't worry about reading a thick book; find something short and directly related to your financial situation).

- Purchase a small filing system and start saving every receipt.
- Each month, calculate your income, and make sure you know where you spend every cent.
- Ask friends about interesting tax breaks they know about or have applied to their income.

Note

1. Diane Kennedy and Garrett Sutton, *Real Estate Loopholes* (New York: Warner Business Books, 2003), 33.

12

INVESTING

Investing money is a beautiful process. Well, I guess it only seems beautiful when you invest in the right thing and see a good return on your funds. Investing means allocating your resources (or somebody else's) into something that will make your money grow . . . usually *with little or no work on your part.* Once you start accumulating some savings in your bank account, you'll need to put it to good work. Turning what money you have into more money is essential to becoming financially wealthy.

It reminds me of planting a seed and watching it turn into a tree. Investments are just that. You put something of value into a system that will cause the worth to increase. A seed goes into the system that consists of nutrient rich soil, water, and sunlight. By the pure nature of the environment that it is placed in, it will either grow or wither up and die. The intelligent caretaker knows proper timing, pruning, and fertilization techniques to ensure speedy and consistent growth. Placing money in the right environment after learning the appropriate caretaker skills is the way people become rich.

A Dollar Today Is Less Tomorrow

It is very important to understand that the value of a dollar diminishes every day. You cannot put $1000 in the bank and expect the value to be the same if you leave it there until retirement. What $1000 buys today will be much more than what it can buy one, five, or ten years from now. $1000 might purchase 500 gallons of gasoline today but only 250 three months from now. I'm sure you understand the process of inflation.

If prices are going up and the money you have in the bank stays the same, you can buy less *unless* you increase the amount of money you have in the bank. While banks will pay you a small percentage of interest for keeping your money there, it doesn't compare to what you can earn by placing your money into other ventures.

The concept of investing is very similar to plain and simple business. You buy something that can be sold immediately or in the future for a higher price than what you paid for it. Most investments, however, deal with property that will appreciate in value. The most popular forms of investing money are in the stock market, real estate, life insurance policies, bonds, or turnkey businesses.

In this chapter we will just cover a couple of these options to give you an idea of what you need to consider once you're earning more money than you're spending. I suggest signing up for the entrepreneur and investing courses offered by Universal Training Center in the Provo area. For a small fee, you can receive in-depth training on how to set up and run a business and attend several seminars from local investors who share their strategies. If you aren't in Provo, you can download the training courses online at www.universaltrainingcenter.com.

Investing in the Stock Market

I'll start off with stocks. The basic concept of buying and selling in the stock market goes as follows: in order to generate more money, large businesses decide to sell ownership of their company to the public, which they divide into stocks. People buy stocks, or a percentage of ownership, in a company if it looks like the business will grow and be profitable. When the business does grow, the value of the stocks they hold increases.

If they bought one thousand shares at ten cents each, and because the company has performed well during the last twelve months and the value has gone up to $1.80 per share, the people have made a good investment. The share holders can then sell their ownership for the market value and reinvest in something that will perform equally well or better. If this particular stock is anticipated to grow even faster in the near future, the share holders would want to wait before selling. In this example a $100 investment was turned into $1,800 over twelve months without the stock holder having to do any work. Not bad, huh? This is just a glorified example, though.

Just as easily, an investor can lose almost everything he puts into the stock market. Say he buys into the same company at $1.80 per share because for the last twelve months the business has done really well and anticipates doing even better the next year. The investor takes a chance and buys up all the shares he can placing his entire $40,000 of savings into this stock. According to many experts, the company looks very promising and should continue to perform well.

Two months later, the stocks are indeed looking great at a value of $2.30 per share, but suddenly there's a recall on the company's entire product line that has been sold for the last year. There was a glitch in the manufacturing that might endanger the lives of their customers. The company tells everyone that it's just a minor technicality and will not affect them in the long run. According to their CFO, the company will recover from this issue in no time and continue to offer the same quality of goods as before. Incidentally, the value of the stocks has already fallen back to $2.10 per share; however, many hang on believing the company will recover and the stocks will take off again.

By this time, the consumer has no trust in this company's product due to harsh media coverage about the recall. Now, the company isn't seeing the sales and profits that they were previously, so many of the stock holders start selling off their shares to recuperate their investment. Supply of these shares goes way up while demand goes way down, and suddenly the stock is worth only $.90 per share.

Now the $40,000 investor has seen his investment diminished down to a value of only $20,000. He can sell out now and try to save what he has left, or he can keep everything and hope that the company will turn around and the stock values will go back up. Stock values go up and down all of the time. He could still possibly turn his $40,000 investment into a profit by hanging on, but he could also lose all $40,000 if the company continues in its downfall.

Many consider the stock market to be risky, but everything in life has risk involved. Even buying a microwave is a risk! You could take it home and find out it doesn't work and then be denied a refund from the store you bought it at. I recently paid six dollars for a movie that stopped working about thirty minutes before the ending . . . the business I bought it from refused to replace it or refund my money. That was a risky investment! If you educate yourself on a subject, you can factor out most of the risk involved and make great money by investing in the stock market. Plenty of low risk stocks are basically guaranteed to go up in value, while many higher risk stocks might boom or might not. How you invest in the stock market is up to you, but it is certainly a way to turn what money you have into much more.

Check out the following websites if you think the stock market is for you: www.wiseoptions.com and www.thinkorswim.com. One of them is a site for buying, trading, and selling stock while the other can provide valuable coaching to direct you towards stock that will perform well. This is one way to play the market without really knowing much about it or having to track the performance of companies.

My brother-in-law was given a small inheritance of $3,000 when he was fifteen years old, which his dad helped him to invest in a certain stock. While he was away on his mission, the stock had appreciated in value so much that he could've cashed out and had $70,000. His father had invested in the same stock and could've cashed out for over $2,000,000! Unfortunately something happened that caused the value of the stocks to take a nose dive. Ten years later, that $3,000 in stocks is now worth $3,000 and still just sitting there.

The fluctuations are mostly unpredictable, but knowing when to buy and sell can realize some of the fastest and easiest money you'll ever obtain. In this case, they didn't sell, because the company made an announcement that they thought would soon increase the value of shares significantly. The $2,000,000 could have turned into $3,000,000 in just a couple of months, but sadly, it didn't.

On the reverse side, a friend of mine who teaches seminary took $10,000 and has turned it into over $50,000 over the last two years just by going to a stock market website and clicking a few buttons once a month. He doesn't really know much about the market, but pays a guy who does to keep track of everything. The fee he pays for this guy's opinion is nothing compared to the returns he has seen on his $10,000 investment.

Investing in Real Estate

Another way to turn your savings into a huge profit is through the real estate industry. America's first millionaire (and soon after multimillionaire) was the son of a butcher with nothing special about his background. He was a trapper who sold furs and traded spices around New York in the 1800s. He then learned how to invest in real estate until he bought and sold most of what is today known as Manhattan Island. When he died, he left an inheritance of over $20,000,000 to his children and grandchildren. In today's money, this was the equivalent of over 500 billion dollars![1]

Real estate is much more stable than the stock market. Throughout history there have been market trends that nearly always go up. Every once in a while there has been a dip in the market, but it's usually very small in comparison with dives in the stock market, and it only lasts a couple of years before beginning to climb back up.

There are countless ways to invest in real estate . . . you can buy raw land, develop it, and sell it; you can buy run-down rental properties to fix up and sell ("flipping" is the terminology used for this strategy in the real estate industry); you can buy "options" to buy properties and resell them before you even own the property. There are myriad opportunities to make money off of real estate, and I mean *big money.*

The great thing about investing in real estate is that you can do it with absolutely no money down. By using other people's money, you can get into rental properties and watch the value of your investment take off as the renters pay for your mortgage. All you have to do is learn how to be a landlord. Real estate can make you wealthier faster than anything else.

There are several ways to get into a property without any money down, but the one you should probably worry about now is known as a conventional loan. More in-depth books about real estate can teach you several financing strategies that involve creative negotiation in order to buy property with no money down.

For now, you can go to a lending agency to speak with a loan officer that can help you understand how to get qualified for a home loan. Mainly lenders want to see a good credit history, so if you don't have a credit card, get one soon. By no means should you run up your bill and accrue debt on your credit card, but use it and pay it off every month. Don't spend on your credit card what you don't have money to pay off by the end of the month. The point of doing this is to build your credit score. You'll need at least three sources of credit to build a good score.

A good credit score will enable you to obtain loans at lower interest rates. It's the first thing any lender looks at to find out their risk in extending you a loan. Late payments and irresponsibility with your debts will ruin your score and cause lenders to reject your loan applications. They will look at your credit score, your debt, your income, your assets, what you want to buy, and how much money you're willing to put down, but their number one priority is lending money to people that will pay it back, so take the necessary steps now to build a high credit rating.

I am a licensed real estate agent/investor and have gained most of my net worth through investing in real estate. During the year 2006, property value in Utah appreciated 23 percent. This means that if you purchased a home for $200,000, it should have been worth around $246,000 by the end of the year. If you bought for under market value (remember that buying low is the key in any transaction) then you made more than the 23 percent increase on your investment. It's actually an infinite increase on your investment considering that you don't pay any of your own money for it if you can finance 100 percent of the purchase price!

The way I structure my dealings in real estate, at the close of a transaction, I actually get paid to buy homes. I also make sure that the rents are high enough to cover my mortgage payment so that tenants pay for my property in exchange for me letting them live there. When it's all said and done, anybody can buy a property for lower than market value with no money of their own, have renters pay for it while the value goes up, and sell for huge profits a few years down the road.

Buying Existing Businesses

Last, buying a turnkey business is something to consider when you have money on hand. Although the business may have the status of a "turnkey" operation, meaning the owner can walk away while the business runs itself, you'll probably find that you have to commit time and energy to it. An unsupervised business is sure to fail. No matter what, you will be emotionally attached to a business if you buy one. Whether or not you buy one depends on the purchase price and potential for profits that the business can provide you. I have friends that bought into a business together and quit their jobs because they could pay themselves more with their own company.

You can often find people desperate to sell and willing to owner-finance an established business. An example is when a man has started up a great business and everything runs exceptionally well, but he unexpectedly passes away and leaves everything to his widow wife. She has no idea how to run it and doesn't want the extra headache, so you can find his store on the market for an incredibly low price. Negotiating good terms for you to take over is usually very easy in situations like this: low or no money down, owner financing at a low interest rate, no payments for the first six months. You get the idea! Keep your eyes open for good deals.

Franchises

Obviously, another business investment option would be a franchise chain. They, more often than not, operate on very efficient systems that can be run by a manager and the employees. Franchises also have an 85 percent success rate, so your chances of making a good profit are much higher than buying out a "mom and pop" organization.

Simply put, buying a franchise is a larger scale investment but a smaller risk. The drawback to this type of investment is the amount of money you pay out of pocket to get started. The franchise fee is normally a large sum of money, and then paying for your location and equipment can drain the bank account quicker than you can get started and see any returns. On top of this, lenders and corporate like to see two to six months of reserves in your bank account to completely sustain your new business for the first little while. This means you need lots of cash to get started. Corporate headquarters of the business also exercises a substantial amount of control over how your franchise is run . . . meaning you're not always your own boss.

Avoid the Naysayers

Many are skeptical of investing and consider it unwise or too risky. I say go for it no matter what your friends or family say! Take your financial advice from millionaires before giving in to the skepticism of those who surround you. I promise you that you'll receive a fair share of pessimistic comments or looks of disapproval. Again, don't let fear dominate your decisions.

Even if you have the worst luck with investing as you begin, life is not over. As mentioned in chapter two, you are young and the time to start is now. If things don't work out, you have plenty of time to recover. The longer you wait to invest, the greater the risk. When you're forty years old, it's much more difficult to crawl out of a financial mistake and not feel it when you retire. You can fall flat on your face as you attempt to invest between the age of twenty-one or thirty, and life goes on. It's much better to have tried and failed than to have never tried at all. At least you will learn and gain experience, and if things actually work out, you can be well on your way to achieving financial freedom.

You need to be willing to take some financial risks in life. I know individuals with hundreds of thousands of dollars in the bank just sitting there earning a whopping 1 to 2 percent return. The bank just takes that money and lends it out at an interest rate of anywhere from 6 percent to 26 percent or higher. If the bank is earning 26 percent returns on your money, so should you!

Compounding your earnings by investing will accumulate much more wealth than just leaving it in a savings account. If you have $100,000 in savings that you invest in something that yields an 8 percent return annually, after three years that money has earned you about $26,000. That's a new car, your child's college education, or money towards the down payment of an investment rental property! If you continue to compound on top of that without pulling out any of your earnings, you will achieve a level of financial wealth that few even dream about.

Let Your Money Do All the Work

The level of financial success that you want to achieve is this: you no longer work for money, because your money works for you! That's right, you can make your money work for you. Learn how to wisely invest your savings, and you'll see enough cash flow profits to pay for all of your bills plus some.

Organize your savings into small categories of investing ventures . . . have some for low-risk investments, some for medium risk, and of course some for high-risk/high-return investments. Please do not risk $8,000 on stocks or a similar investment unless you can live without the $8,000. It's not like the movies where you spend your last five dollar bill on some lottery tickets and become an instant millionaire.

Controlling your pools of money so that their operations bring in enough profit to provide you and your family a comfortable life while earning extra that you can reinvest is an accomplishment you should work towards. Please reread that last sentence until you understand exactly what I'm saying. This is the ultimate level of freedom that you absolutely deserve! Can you break away from the traditions of society and make it happen? The most effective way to learn about investing is by actually doing it.

Exercise:

1) Buy a small seed for a pea plant (easy to maintain and fruit-bearing). Find a small pot, add some soil, bury your seed, give it a little water, and place it by a window where it can get

plenty of sunshine. Why? This will be your daily reminder about the principle of investing. Every day you see how a small seed can be converted into a towering, fruit bearing plant, you'll be reminded that your money could be and should be doing the exact same thing. Take care of your plant . . . it's good practice

2) Choose one of the three investment strategies listed above and learn how you can begin immediately. If you choose stocks, start off small. If you choose real estate, learn this month how you can get into your first property. If you opt to buy a business, start searching the classifieds and look for owner financing. Don't cheat yourself with an attitude that investing can wait until you've begun a career. Investing might become your career!

Note

1. Gary Keller, *The Millionaire Real Estate Investor* (New York:McGraw-Hill, 2005), 123.

13

The Power of Leverage

As you enter the world of investments and building wealth, it won't take long for you to understand clearly the concept of leverage. Most of those go-getters out there making the big bucks are doing it with opium! Not really opium, but OPM, or "other people's money."

I hate to state the obvious, but I'd rather not pass up a good opportunity to employ a little visual. *Leverage* is derived from the same word as *lever*. See the following visual if you need a reminder of what a lever actually is:

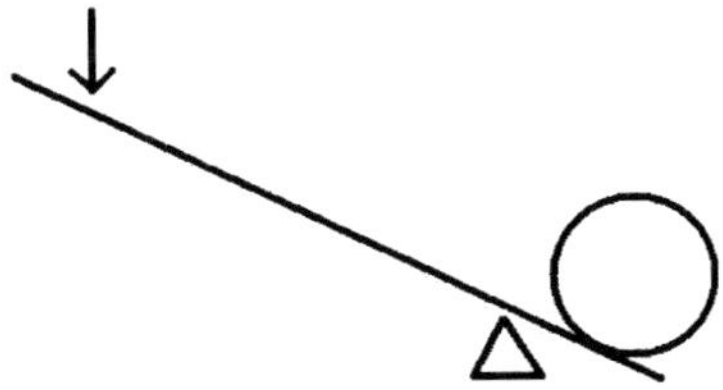

One of the world's greatest gifts was brought to us by the power of leverage. That's right—Joseph Smith unearthed the magnificent golden plates that were destined to change the world with the help of a long stick he used as a lever. His own strength wasn't enough to remove the heavy rock that hid the ancient record, but with the right tool Joseph uncovered the most important book in the history of mankind. Just as Joseph Smith was guided to a treasure of infinite value, we can use the principle of leverage in this life to find a pile of gold.

In the world of investments and finance, *leverage* means the ability to obtain funds that you can invest and generate a profitable return on your investment. The power to use OPM to earn money for yourself is a pearl of great price. You can be broke and busted but still have the ability to earn hundreds of thousands of dollars per year.

Use Your Money to Leverage More

A quick example: Johnny B. Goodman has $10,000 saved up in the bank and finds a great rental property being sold for $15,000 less than market value that he would like to finance. He goes to the bank and says, "I'd like to use your money to buy a rental property." The bank says, "We'd be happy to give you OPM as long as you pay us 7 percent interest on it and amortize the note over a thirty-year period. The only thing you need to do is show us a high credit score and be willing to make a down payment of 5 percent of the property cost." This means Johnny can use his $10,000 to leverage $190,000 and buy his property that might appreciate at 14 percent annually over the next four or five years, and his tenants will pay his mortgage for him.

His monthly payment that the bank charges is $1300, but he rents the property out for $1500 per month and raises rents 5 percent each year. Johnny B. Goodman paid $10,000 to access OPM, but every month for the next five years, he made an average of $375 per month in rental cash flow, which adds up to over $20,000. When you calculate the tax advantages he received for paying interest and consider the appreciation factor, Johnny was sitting pretty because his property was now worth over $100,000 more than what he paid for it five years before and he had saved somewhere in the neighborhood of $20,000 in taxes. Add it all up and you'll see that Johnny B. Goodman was sitting on top of the world, because he had turned his $10,000 into over $140,000 in five years by leveraging the bank's money and just finding tenants to occupy his property. All he had to do was mow the lawn from time to time . . . not to mention he got his original $10,000 deposit back when he sold the property.

Using Equity to Leverage

Randy C. Greatly had a slightly more aggressive investment strategy with his money and saw similar results by using OPM. He actually had no money! Zip, zilch, nada. He did, however, have a phenomenally high credit score but that was it. Randy was self-employed and couldn't show on his tax returns what kind of money he had available to live off of, because business owners take advantage of so many tax breaks that it actually looks like they don't earn very much on their tax forms (lenders always want to see these documents as proof of income). Because of his credit score, the bank told Randy "We'll give you access to OPM, but you'll have to pay a little bit more interest on whatever we give you." Randy said, "Hey, that's fine. I can use your money to make way more than what I'm going to have to pay you for it. If I can earn 20 percent returns on that money and only have to pay you 8.5 percent for it, I'm ready to go."

Randy bought the same type of property that Johnny had invested in. He, also, was very smart about buying a property that was underpriced. Since he was paying higher interest rates to use OPM, he wasn't able to cash flow very much, if any, off of the monthly rents that were paid to him. But he realized pretty soon that the property he purchased had appreciated over $30,000 during the first year that he owned it.

A book Randy was reading taught him about how easy it was to "refinance" a home and borrow the equity you have in the property (equity simply means the difference in what the property is worth and what you owe on it). The next week, he set up an appointment with a loan officer, and they applied for a Home Equity Line of Credit (HELOC). Within two weeks he was given a $25,000 line of credit, which he used to do two things. He used $5,000 to remodel his property a little and add more value to it, and he used $15,000 to leverage financing for another rental property. It was easy to access OPM when he showed up with a high credit score and 5 percent to 10 percent cash to put down for a new loan.

Within five years, Randy owned twelve different rental properties that were receiving approximately $600 per month total. The amazing part is that he had over $300,000 in equity between the twelve units. He could either continue to sell or refinance his properties and leverage more of OPM to grow his portfolio of rental properties, or he could be content with what he had and just wait for the mortgages to pay for themselves and retire off of the rental income. I hope he continues to multiply his investments with the power of leverage that he understands so well.

Both guys here used the principle of leverage to earn an impressive amount of net worth, but Randy compounded his efforts to earn about three times more than Johnny. In the investing game, leverage really is the key to success. Doing whatever it takes to access OPM at interest rates far lower than the returns you can earn with it is vital to a rich man's success.

Leverage Essentials

What does it take to leverage money? Keep five things in mind:

1) High credit score. Low credit will virtually ruin your chances of accessing OPM, because lenders will think that it's too risky to lend to a person that can't be responsible about paying back his or her debts. Protect your credit and learn how to raise it to over seven hundred points. Pay all of your bills on time, because creditors can report your late payments to the credit bureaus, and it will destroy your score. One late payment could ruin your chances of leveraging money for the deal of a lifetime. Also, keep your credit card balances low (try not to spend more than 30 percent to 40 percent of your limit).

2) Documented income. Having a steady income is very important, but there are lenders that will do stated income loans (meaning you just verbally tell them what you make, and they don't need documentation to verify). W-2 forms that show your yearly earnings are the most important, but when you hold a full-time job, a simple paycheck stub from a recent month is enough to leverage the financing you need. They will compare your income to your debts and analyze a "debt-to-income ratio." They usually want to see that your debt payments are less than half of your income after they add the debt payments to your proposed monthly mortgage payment.

3) Assets. These aren't completely necessary to have, but lenders like to know that they can "secure" their loans with something of value . . . meaning that if you don't pay them back, they can take your assets from you to compensate for their losses. When you have properties, savings, or stocks, they feel safer about lending to you.

4) Money in the bank and money to use as a down payment. Lenders like to see that you have enough cash to pay several months of whatever your monthly bills will be. They will also require you often times to invest your own money on deals (3 to 20 percent usually). One hundred percent loans are available, without a doubt, but they will certainly have higher interest rates to be paid and are more difficult to qualify for.

5) Value in your investments. Banks want to own loans . . . not homes. Since they risk having to foreclose and take over title to a property if the borrower doesn't pay his note, they make sure not to lend out more money than the property is really worth. An appraisal showing that the home is valued at what you're paying for it will always be necessary. They won't just give you money without knowing that they are protected, so be prepared for that part of the process. You can't get a $200,000 loan for a property that is only worth $180,000 (no matter how much you like the property). There are some situations where lenders will actually give you 105 percent of the property's value or maybe more, but in general, the loan terms aren't that appealing.

If you need to leverage money for a business project, a business plan that outlines exactly how you will earn money and repay the loan will be required. They will want to secure the loan by the value of your inventory or your business itself. The underlying factor of everything is to provide security to the lender in case you decide to stop paying them back for the money they lend you.

Only Borrow to Invest

Realistically, anybody can leverage money. This is very different from building frivolous debt. Buying a used car on borrowed money is not leverage unless, for some weird reason, the value of the car goes up, or you're using the car to produce an income. Leveraging OPM in order to make wise investments will earn you considerably more than what you are paying in interest—it is a sure way to become a millionaire.

The sooner you can shape your loan application resumé into what looks like a safe and protected investment for banks, the more money you will retire with. Focus on the five factors and you will see how easy it is to access OPM. You will always find investments that basically require your brain power along with the willingness to walk over to a bank and apply for a loan. Doing enough projects with OPM will ensure the extra income that everybody longs for and will allow you to live comfortably.

Why You Must Not Fear Good Debt

Past generations have been afraid of mortgages and preach against having debt built into your homes. This attitude dates back to the times of the Great Depression. Lenders often included a clause in lending contracts that enabled them to call the loan due at any time—they could take homes if people couldn't pay the full amount. With the crash of the stock market and people losing their jobs, banks started repossessing millions of homes. Even people with only a small amount left to pay off lost everything. Since this happened, generations from 1930 to around 1970 have believed that a mortgage is a necessary evil, and that you should pay it off as soon as possible.

Most of America's richest men today have more than enough money to pay off their house, but they don't because they can use that money to make more money. Surely there's a point you reach where you want to guarantee the security of having a home for you and your family by paying it off, but that'll be for you to decide when you get there. I won't bore you with the number details, but the difference between two men with the same income and the same amount of savings who pay their mortgages differently can result in a drastically different outcome. The man who pays it off in fifteen years and applies all of his extra income to paying it off as soon as possible and then starts investing at age 45 will normally end up with over $500,000 less than the man who pays off his home in thirty years and conservatively invests the difference on the side until he's sixty. The more cash you have, the more OPM you will be able to access and profit from.

Use Creativity to Leverage

Banks aren't the only sources of money out there. There are tons and tons of home owners willing to carry a note and "seller finance" a property. Most often, you can negotiate better terms (interest rate, monthly payments, life of the loan, balloon payments, and so on). Wise investors learn creative ways to find financing and leverage the money they need to score big on investment opportunities. I recommend reading Robert Allen's book called *Nothing Down for the 2000s.*

In this chapter, I spoke mainly about leveraging funds for rental properties, but there are many other applications of this principle. Successful people leverage OPM for their businesses, to develop raw land, to build shopping malls, to buy stocks, and so forth. Whatever you choose to invest in, leverage will help you see more profit for your efforts.

This could very possibly be the most significant wealth-building principle you will ever learn. Without access to funding, the income process is slow and painful. Imagine having to work until you've saved up hundreds of thousands of dollars so you can begin investing. By the time you earned enough to see a decent return on investment, you'd be wanting to spend all of your savings on your failing health. If you get anything out of this book, I hope it is an understanding of the power of leverage and a desire to focus on the five factors that determine your ability to leverage. Remember, OPM is your lever tool that will allow you to unearth a pile of gold.

EXERCISE:

Go speak with two or three loan officers and find out if you qualify for a home loan. Even if you don't, it's good to know why you don't and what you need to work towards. The loan officer will pull your credit score, analyze your debt-to-income ratios, and check to see if any programs are available to assist you in an investment. Don't have more than two or three pull your credit score, because the credit bureaus will knock several points off of your score for repeatedly checking (they see that you are looking for a loan and lower your score to prevent consumer debt).

Learn at least one technique for negotiating a seller finance note on something that requires a loan. This is the more creative part of leveraging, and if learned, will be the most beneficial in building your investment portfolio. Even if you qualify with banks and their strict lending guidelines, you will one day reach a limit where the banks will start to say no. Knowing how to create owner finance purchases will open up doors without end.

14

Saving Up

In a perfect world, you are already a brilliant budget manager who knows how to control your precious money. All missionaries receive their monthly stipends, which should be just enough to scrape by on when supporting a very modest lifestyle. For most, not spending your monthly allowance wisely could lead to some real problems, so a typical missionary should return home understanding the concept of money management.

Unfortunately, money donations from friendly members or loved ones result in a larger than necessary balance from time to time. Didn't you just hate it when you had extra money? Yeah, me too! Others get stuck with companions that blow all their money before the month is over and have to kindly share their own funding. Ain't life grand! You come across extra cash here and there that you put away hoping to buy something nice, and before you know it, you're having to spend your reserves unexpectedly on things that you really don't want to splurge on.

It's always amazed me to know that missionaries have come home with thousands and thousands of dollars saved up. Ending your mission with enough cash to buy yourself a brand new car shouldn't really be happening, but it does and I gotta tell ya—I'm impressed! I'm not saying that it's a sin to end up with extra spending money as a missionary. Most of the time, you don't really have much control over what amount of donations come your way. I've yet to come across a rule that dictates whether you should save any funds when possible. There are those who buy new suits and ties every month, and there are those who hold onto every little nickel and dime.

I'll be the first to admit . . . I learned a bare minimum about money management during my mission. In Peru, every American dollar I had to my name was really like having 3.5 times its value. I had access to my $1500 that I had saved up from high school graduation gifts, and my parents made sure to send me a $20 bill with every other letter they wrote me. Most of my budget was spent on traveling from one appointment to another, but I definitely made sure that my companion and I got a really nice meal with each $20 I got in the mail. I still managed to drop from 175 pounds to a scrawny 135 before coming home, so maybe you understand why I welcomed the opportunity for fine dining every once in a while.

For the first month of my mission, I didn't spend a single centavo (cent) on anything unnecessary. After my first zone meeting where we took a break and I saw other missionaries buying cookies and soda, my jaw about hit the ground. At that point, the thought of buying something for myself hadn't even crossed my mind. What a revelation!

With the arrival of a new mission president though, our budget was cut significantly and money became a real problem for most missionaries. I recall every missionary in one of my zones being completely out of money halfway through the month. When I was serving as a zone leader, we were given a monthly sum that was completely depleted after the first week when it was spent on absolutely nothing but missionary work. Luckily, the access to my bank account in Texas helped us do effectively everything that we needed to do. Most of the money went towards taxi fees to get us around our immense areas (no bikes or cars for the missionaries in South America, and walking to some appointments would have taken several hours). The mission president was bent on maintaining the new budget plan he had established, so we had no choice but to survive with what we were given.

Ultimately, it worked out fine, and my mission experience helped me learn to allocate my funds wisely. However, working on an insufficient budget and being able to access more money than I really needed made it hard to learn about saving. Just because I didn't learn much about saving in the mission doesn't mean I couldn't figure out the concept somehow or another. Everybody has to save for that pair of shoes, designer purse, or shotgun he or she wants. As you get older, it's the cars, houses, and vacations that you save up for mostly, but the fundamental principle is the same. This is a very important concept that must be mastered if you have any hopes of being successful in this life.

Some might disagree, but my philosophy is that you can't save money unless you're earning enough to pay all your bills . . . *and some.* I've seen teachings that you should save a portion of your income no matter what, and you'll realize that what you think is impossible really isn't. I'm sorry to tell you that if your monthly income is $3,000 dollars and your food, housing, transportation, phone, entertainment, and everything else in your budget is equal to about $3,000 dollars, you won't see any savings until you increase your income.

Hang on to Your Savings

Once you figure out a way to earn a little more than you spend on a monthly basis, the trick is to *not spend the extra*! You'll hear this over and over about mankind—"limited means and unlimited wants." It really is a truth about our nature. We have our income spent before we actually have the money earned. The excess cash starts burning a hole in our pockets before it even gets there.

The best way to avoid spending frivolously is to set investment goals. Know that you need about 10–20 percent down to buy an investment property, find a price range that works for your plans, and start saving up until you reach that 10 or 20 percent marker. There are thousands of things you can save up for, but the purpose of this chapter is not to instruct on the "what" but more on the "how." Define something to save for and get started. Once you stash your money into a savings account, leave it there until you reach your goal no matter what.

Goal Saving

Before continuing on about strategies for saving money, allow me to clarify the importance of saving for something specific and something intelligent. Saving for assets and not liabilities should always be your main objective. An asset is something that will make money for you because it increases in value while a liability is the exact opposite. A house would be an asset, because it will appreciate in value. A car is usually a liability because it depreciates and costs you money for gas, maintenance, and insurance non-stop. Fancy TVs, stereos, new clothes, or motorcycles shouldn't be on your list of things to save up for just yet.

I'm not saying that you should never save up for toys and the fun things in life, but the bulk of your savings should go towards building your asset portfolio. If you do this effectively, you'll be able to afford all of the hot rods and dream vacations a lifetime can handle.

Now, you've established your monthly expenses and know that your lifestyle requires a minimum of let's say $2,700 each month to squeak by. You are up to $3,500 net income per month and know that you have to be smart with the extra money. After tithing you have a total of $450 to spare. If you are dead set on achieving financial stability as soon as possible you will take all $450 and deposit it into a savings account ASAP. You will also realize that if you find additional ways to earn income on the side (mowing lawns, pouring concrete, buying and selling junk) you could easily deposit an extra $500–$1000 dollars each month into your savings.

Within a year or two, it should be pretty easy to take your money out of a savings account that pays 3 percent and into an investment that pays you 20 percent returns. Saving like this isn't easy and requires a lot of discipline, but it's well worth the pain and agony that we go through when our extra money is begging us to waste it on the moment.

Save Enough and Don't Be Afraid to Invest

Please understand that saving money is absolutely worthless if you don't intend to invest it and realize larger returns than what the bank will pay you. Why give them your money that they pay you 3 percent for while they lend it out to the world for 10 percent? If you can't find ways to earn more than 3 percent returns on your savings, then you don't deserve to see it grow any faster than it will.

Some people do put their money in the bank and leave it there for the remainder of their lives. Very few of these people actually become millionaires because the increments are too small to see any significant growth, but they could've turned it into several million if not billions much quicker by using it to invest. In summary, save until you have enough to invest and then INVEST! It makes no sense to not make your money work for you, unless you are already filthy rich with no need to worry about an increase.

Discipline to Save

Let's tackle the tricky part of actually disciplining yourself in the art of saving money. Earlier, I said that you can take every extra dollar you earn and start building up your savings account, but that's not always the most enjoyable way to live life. Start off by saving 5 percent of each paycheck and see how well you do. After a couple of months surviving, increase the percentage that you deposit into savings. Soon, you'll want to be up to at least 10 percent of your monthly income being saved for investment purposes. I invite you to set a goal of saving between 15 and 20 percent of your wages.

The way to make sure this is doable is to keep your monthly expenses to a minimum. Don't start buying things you don't really need until you can afford them. The new car with its $500 monthly installment and $150 insurance premium can wait until you are well on your way to financial wealth. Drive that hunker into the ground and then stick to the cheap, used cars that won't drain your monthly cash flow. The daily junk food and fast food restaurants will add up to hundreds of dollars you could've saved at the end of the month. Keeping your monthly bills lower means that you will have serious investment cash much sooner. The more investment funds you build, the faster you will reach an early retirement.

How can you be certain that each and every month you successfully put back the 10 percent that you already committed to saving? Once you have that money in your hand, it just kicks and screams and begs you to go spend it. Flashes of fancy furniture, the latest CDs, or mouthwatering restaurants start popping up in your mind, and you really want to reward yourself. "What will one time hurt?" you ask. It requires some steadfast determination to make it to the bank and deposit the full 10 percent into your savings account.

Automatic Deposits

You can take a few different approaches. The first one is, by far, the easiest and doesn't require much discipline to make certain you don't falter. All it takes is an automatic deposit system that most employers offer. If you can accept your paycheck through a direct deposit, this is the most effective way to proceed with the savings process.

All you have to do is provide your employer with your bank account information and you will never even see your paycheck, because it will electronically transfer into your account without you ever touching it. If this system is possible, a short appointment with your bank will allow you to arrange for the 10 percent to be taken from each paycheck and deposited in your savings account. Voilá! What you don't see, you won't want to spend.

If you're an entrepreneur making out your own paychecks or if your place of employment simply doesn't offer the direct deposit service, you'll need to be a little more disciplined. With each trip to the bank for a deposit, you'll have to manually fill out the deposit slip directing the appropriate amount into your savings account.

If you don't trust that you can accomplish this every time, hold yourself accountable with the help of your spouse, a friend, or even an accountant. Make sure they understand what your goals are and take a look at your accounts each month to verify that you're actually doing what you're supposed to. You might even want to become friends with a banker and ask him or her to hold you accountable for depositing the appropriate amount into your savings account with each trip to the bank.

An excellent, inspirational story might help you understand the importance of saving. A man who lived in a world where it was hard to earn a living became one of the richest men to ever walk the earth. The book titled *The Richest Man in Babylon* by George S. Clason will take you on an inspirational journey with a man who doesn't manage money very well and accumulates too much debt. His transformation in financial strategy and motivation, which led him to prosperity, could possibly open your eyes and teach you a path to debt-free living with money to spare. I highly recommend giving it a read. It won't take you very long to finish the book since it is fairly short.

EXERCISE:

First thing's first—set an investment goal. I suggest something small if you are living on a pretty tight budget. Save enough to buy and flip an underpriced motorcycle, garden tiller, television, or piece of furniture. Pick something that you understand and study the market for a few weeks as you save up. There are classified ads everywhere that you can use for this exercise. Beware: Flipping something like this for a profit is addictive and could result in excess riches! Know what a good deal is and define exactly how much you will need to save up for that bargain.

You'll need to save enough money that you can invest to make \$100-\$500 dollars on one deal. To do this, you will most likely need to save between \$300 and \$1,000 dollars. I've bought aquariums for \$300 dollars that I sold for \$1,000 within one week of posting an ad. I've bought dogs from owners who couldn't handle them and resold them for more than a \$750 profit. I'll pick up things under the *free* category of the classifieds and make \$300 bucks off of them within a week. Choose two or three different things and know exactly how much you will need to save to get your foot into a deal.

Once you define your savings goal, start putting back whenever possible. You might even sell off some of your unwanted junk to speed up the process. As you near the marker on your savings goal, start putting in low-ball offers (it's a fact that you will receive a discount most of the time when you just ask), but invest wisely in something you are certain that you can resell quickly. Getting stuck with something that isn't in very high demand and that you can't use isn't a great way to start investing.

Once you reach your first milestone in investment savings, set higher goals. Save up $10,000 for the stock market; $25,000 to buy a turnkey business; and $100,000 to leverage a $1,000,000 commercial property.

Saving for investments is fundamental and absolutely necessary in the wealth building process. The sooner you can master this principle and define your necessary savings amounts, the sooner you will have the means to exponentially turn your money into more. While saving might seem like a sacrifice, you will reap the benefits for a lot longer than not spending that money.

15

Ten Ways to Waste Your Time

"I was supposed to get up and find a job today, but by the time I woke up it was way too late. I know it ain't right to procrastinate, so I swear I'll start tomorrow, but today it can wait. If there's one thing that I notice about time, no matter how hard you kill it, it won't die."[1]

Adapting to Normal Life

Not many people talk about the greeny phase after the mission. You remember all the ancient missionaries you met right when you arrived to the field? They had about one month or two to three weeks left, and they just looked at you and laughed. Not that they were picking on you or anything . . . you just totally reminded them of how long they had been in the mission field and how far along they had come. Little did you know that there's a very similar stage when you return home. People will look at you and just laugh for reasons beyond your comprehension.

It probably varies on where you end up after your mission, but if you live in a predominantly LDS area where returned missionaries abound, you'll know exactly what I'm talking about. It's like you become a social rookie the minute you take off your name tag and start dating again.

I know that I had a date lined up the night after I got back, and all I did was show pictures and talk about Peru. Most who are fresh off the mission have no clue that it isn't the most exciting thing for girls to date all of these returned missionaries who do nothing but ramble on about converts and companions from the last two years. It's difficult for people who weren't there to relate to the conversation. I heard about what a *faux pas* it was to dwell on the mission around other people and concluded that it was somewhat sacrilegious and hypocritical to criticize others for sharing about their mission experience. My thoughts—I loved my mission and if I had comments about it, I'd make them. I have a brother-in-law who has been home for two years now, and I have yet to be around him without hearing mention of something about his mission in Canada.

Maintain Your Habits of Productivity

You know a returned missionary is still in the greeny phase when he's sticking to the missionary routine. I hear about it all of the time and think that it's fantastic: waking up at 6:00 am every day to do your scripture study even though you don't have class or work until 9:00 or 10:00. Some people do it, because they are morning people who prefer to study in the mornings. Many do it out of missionary habit. I respect that and think that it's a great schedule to follow. It might drive your roommates a little crazy, but I find it to be very admirable. Personally, I spent the first six weeks after my mission catching up on all of the sleep I had missed out on during the previous two years. Not recommendable, but no regrets on my part. I'm a night owl . . . you'd laugh if you knew at what hours the pages of this book were written.

The issue I'm trying to address is that missionaries don't waste time in the field. Every minute of every day is planned with two or three back-up plans in case the original falls through (which is usually the case). Missionary productivity is phenomenal compared to what the ordinary person accomplishes on a daily basis. Very few people are disciplined enough to take advantage of the precious time a day has to offer. Suddenly, when we come back to the world of college, work, and dating, our productivity plunges. We quickly relearn the familiar habit of wasting time.

This chapter will point out a few of the major ways a returned missionary can waste valuable time. The time that, if used wisely, could determine your financial prosperity in the future. Make a decision now to balance your schedule and not get caught up doing brainless activities that do not help you progress.

Playing Video Games

I've never been a big Nintendo buff, but I did get caught up in an intense video game right after I moved into my college apartment. My roommate was a good friend of mine who grew up about twenty minutes down the road from my home town, but we didn't meet until we were serving in the same mission together. He finished up before I did, so when I came home from the mission I gave him a call to find out about BYU housing. I was invited to come live with him in his apartment and graciously accepted. The very first night, I was cordially introduced to his Xbox and a little game called *Halo.*

After traveling more than thirty hours on the road from Texas to Utah, I was quite exhausted and just wanted a bed to crash on. Around midnight, I tucked myself in while my roommate continued playing his video game in the living room. The next morning I woke up to find him zonked out in the very same spot he was at when I went to bed. With the game controller still in his hand, he was sprawled out on the floor and against the couch with the TV and Xbox still running. That was enough for me to decide that I wouldn't waste any of my time playing those mind-numbing video games.

Unfortunately, he made me sit down and give it a try one day, and to my surprise, it was kind of fun! For the next nine months, the Elders' quorum in that student ward wasted hours and hours every week playing *Halo.* Just about every apartment had an Xbox, and we could link up our systems to play tournaments with sixteen people at a time. It was a weekly ritual to open all of our doors and run our wires upstairs and down so we could wage electronic warfare on each other. The ridiculous part is how the beautiful girls in the ward would come over to watch us play, and we'd keep our eyes glued to the TV screens without even acknowledging their presence.

I received a video game console for Christmas the next year (even though I still wasn't a big fan of playing video games). I used it every so often to play the one game that I liked, but other than that, it was only played by my roommates. And, when I say it was used by roommates, I'm talking all day long. I had a roommate who would go rent a video game every other week and spend the next seven days trying to beat the game. I timed him on one occasion, and to my disbelief, he played a video game for fourteen hours straight. Besides the brief bathroom breaks and a meal or two, he was stuck inside the world of video games while taking no classes and living off of borrowed money.

My advice: don't own a video game console, and if you live with somebody who does, limit your time on it. M. Russell Ballard said it well when he asked, "What will you say to the Lord when He asks what you have done with the precious gift of life and time? Surely you will not feel comfortable telling Him that you were able to pass the 100,000-point level in a challenging video game."[2] I'm not saying you can't play video games at all. You need playtime, and if enjoying video games is a good pastime for you, then have fun with it here and there. If you're spending more than a few hours every week with your head buried in the TV screen and a controller in your hand, get away from it. I sold my console after about six months . . . not because I had a problem with it, but because my roommate would've rotted away on the couch if I had let him.

Playing Sports Excessively

Sports are a blessing. I love going out and competing every once in a while in just about any sport that was ever invented (except for figure skating). This morning, as a matter of fact, I played a round of golf and scored better than I ever have in my whole life. It's a great way for me to take a load off and clear my mind. Mastering your motor and mental skills is a challenging, yet rewarding part of having a physical body.

In my experience, I've seen acquaintances spend way too much time trying to develop athletic talents with no particular end to justify their actions. If you're looking for an athletic scholarship or just need to stay in shape, practicing sports is okay. I know individuals who aren't willing to work or who lose focus on their education because of some competitive obsession with sports. Again, if your skills are going to pay off with collegiate scholarships or could possibly land you a position with the pros, spending more time playing sports is justified. But spending hours a day playing sports for no particular reason other than the satisfaction of competing can be a waste of time.

Likewise, following sports on TV can be a huge distraction from more important things you could be doing. Watching the ESPN highlights every day to follow the scores of your favorite NFL, NBA, or MBA teams is pointless. Worse than that is watching the full games on all of the sports channels. I'm not saying that enjoying sports is evil! I'm just stating that dedicating too much time to observing muscle maniacs run a football up and down a field as they try to clobber each other will do nothing to help you build a savings account. Play sports and watch sports . . . just evaluate how much time you're dedicating to something that will yield little or no results.

The Internet

Where should I start with the Internet? There is virtually no limit to what you could waste your time on when you have a high speed Internet connection (and practically every little corner of the world has an Internet hub these days). There are those who are literally addicted to the Internet with life-destroying vices and habits that Satan has established for dragging souls down to hell.

Various ways to waste time online: chatting, gambling, playing games, watching TV, shopping, blogging, viewing pornographic materials, dating websites, video sharing, reading e-books, or just clicking buttons to see where you might end up.

Of course, the Internet is a marvelous invention with the technology to do so much good, but there are definitely too many ways to waste quality time with it. The Internet is a vital part of any business' operations, so spending time online is a necessity in today's world of money. The problem arises when we get distracted by the several activities I listed above. Some of the things I listed are certainly okay to do, and you don't have to worry about losing your temple recommend over it. I only suggest that you be concerned about how much time you dedicate to your Internet activity. Are you watching online episodes of your favorite show, one after another, all day to the point where you aren't focusing on other, more productive activities?

Or are you risking your chastity and worthiness by visiting pornographic websites (or any website where the devil posts his evil snares)? Be extremely careful about the way you surf the Internet. Many websites seem harmless, but Satan inevitably finds a way to put offensive and obscene materials right in front of your eyes when you're trying your best to avoid the temptations. Always keep your computer in a public environment, and never, ever set up your laptop or desktop in an office or corner of a room where others can't view your screen openly.

Use the technology of the Internet to your advantage. Be productive and efficient with the time you spend visiting other websites or building your own. I believe that knowing how to use the Internet is one of the surest ways to build a small fortune. But wasting your precious time day after day, consumed by one or more of the activities listed in this section, can be detrimental to your ambitions.

Cell Phones

With current technology, you can do anything you want from the tiny cell phone that fits into your pocket. Cellular phones not only allow you to talk to anybody you want, anywhere in the world, but now, you can watch TV, surf the Internet, listen to music, send text messages, or play games all day long. It really amazes me how far we've advanced from the simple concept of a portable telephone. While the technology is impressive, most of it is far from necessary.

Let me be the first to admit that I've wasted too many hours because of all of the gadgets programmed into my cell phone. Luckily, you can erase the games off of most phones that are being made these days. I seriously don't want to even know how many wasted days I spent on my phone if I calculated all the times I played this simplistic electronic card game I had. After a self-evaluation of time proficiency, I refuse to download songs, games, or any other time waster onto my cell phone. If it's not being used as a tool for communication, chances are, it's not being used wisely.

Reading Junk Literature

Maybe I'm biased on this issue, but I've never really grasped the point or benefit of reading your ordinary fictional literature. Yes, I agree that many fictional works have played important roles throughout history. I know how Chaucer and his *Canterbury Tales* helped solidify English as a language, and I know how Shakespeare with his masterful works was just as important. I'm aware of the influence that art, including literature, has had on the cultural progress of every nation known to mankind. I cannot deny, however, that I don't feel that I've gained valuable knowledge after reading *most* fictional literature.

I'm not counseling anybody not to read fiction. I believe that many authors have given the world treasures of entertainment, which I am grateful for in my life. There are works that can be inspiring and educational. I am saying, however, that I prefer watching the movie when one is available. I'm not really a slow reader, but I know I'm committing to around twenty or more hours of flipping through an average book's pages when I pick it up for a read. That's a lot of time that I could use to do other things when there's a two-hour movie that I can rent or check out at the library. Yes, I'm aware that the movies can be different from the books, but I'm willing to sacrifice a little quality here and there if it saves me time. You know how the saying goes: "Time is money!" Be your own judge when it comes to what literature is beneficial and what literature is absorbing your time for no good reason. Might as well be watching some soap operas as far as I'm concerned, if you're content with reading a pointless romance novel for hours and hours.

Sleeping and Relaxing

Health experts say an adult needs seven to eight hours of sleep every night to live a healthy life. I'm an eight-hour kind of guy. I can get by on six hours, but I'm definitely not the perkiest when I lose out on my full eight hours. Anything less than six hours and I obsess with the thought of getting my needed sleep all day long. About once a week, I indulge and sleep in an extra hour, which I don't usually regret.

Do you know anybody who sleeps more than eight or nine hours a day? Yeah, the person who wakes up after noon every day. That's not you is it? If so, the time has come to change things up a little . . . if you really wish to be successful. If you don't care that much, then keep on sleeping, but know that the money you dream about won't become a reality unless you open your eyes and earn it.

Some people operate on a different schedule—going to bed later than most and sleeping a full eight hours. Winston Churchill, one of the world's greatest leaders, usually worked all hours of the night and then slept in late. If this is you, it'll probably all change when you start having kids and have to adjust to their schedules, but for now, as long as you're not sleeping too much, don't beat yourself up over what time you do what.

Many people get plenty of sleep at night, but when they get home from work, they turn off their brains, turn on their TVs, and slouch down in the recliner until they fall asleep for a nap. Being lethargic around the home when your work is done is not a good habit to get into. I learned a very important lesson from my father in high school as I came home from basketball practice every day and made it a custom of falling asleep on the couch. After a couple of weeks, he started waking me up and saying, "Son, that is not a good habit to get into. Get off your butt and do something worth while."

Getting more sleep than needed can actually make you feel just as crummy as not getting enough. Watch yourself in your sleeping/relaxing habits. Sleeping is a must, but I can't think of one way you can progress when you're snoozing.

2 Nephi 1:13: "O that ye would awake; awake from a deep sleep, yea, even from the sleep of hell, and shake off the awful chains by which ye are bound, which are the chains which bind the children of men, that they are carried away captive down to the eternal gulf of misery and woe."

Hanging Out

Talking the talk without walking the walk—the epidemic that plagues people of all ages. It's interesting to think about how much of my time was wasted in exploring ideas and chitchatting about whose philosophies and theories concerning money or relationships were best. I recall talking for hours about how to get the girl while those most adamant about their own strategies never seemed to actually land a girlfriend . . . maybe that's just because they were picky (sarcasm). I honestly wasted a few too many nights hanging out with buddies (male and female) just shooting the breeze about how much better life was going to be when we figured out the right way to go about things. Little did I realize how much better life would be when I actually *did* something instead of just theorizing on how to do it.

I remember the summer semesters, when the majority of the BYU students would go home to their parents, or they would leave town to go earn their tuition money. It seemed like I spent the majority of my evenings just hanging out with friends and waiting for the time to pass. The conversations inevitably led to the same redundant topics day after day. We always rambled on about relationships and our financial visions. There came a point when I got sick of talking about it and decided that I was going to make something happen. By understanding that hanging out just to run my mouth or listen to somebody else was a waste of time, I became more productive in my day-to-day activities.

Social activity is one of the most influential factors that affect our level of happiness, so hang out with friends and loved ones and have a good time with them. Don't ever let somebody tell you that there's no time to socialize. Just make sure you're not spending hours and hours engaging in conversations that aren't beneficial to you and your plans. Hanging out with friends every evening with nothing on the agenda could be detrimental to your financial goals, so organize your time accordingly. Don't make it a habit of doing nothing for hours.

Recently, I can think of at least eight hours that my wife and I spent hanging out with friends on three different occasions. We love the time we spend with them and have a blast when we're together, but eight hours of my week playing games and talking could have been cut in half, and I would have felt better about myself. Had we spent a little less time just hanging out and focused on being more productive, we would have been able to accomplish our goals much sooner.

The slogan for the first Labor Day parade in 1882 was "eight hours of work, eight hours of rest, eight hours for what we will." This might have been inspired by the Prophet Brigham Young's motto "eight hours work, eight hours sleep, and eight hours recreation."[3] This should be the eleventh commandment and fourteenth article of faith, if you ask me. Don't take away from your play time, and don't become a robot obsessed with your own agenda of prosperity. Hanging out with friends and family will bring you some of the best memories this life has to offer, but remember to be moderate in how much time you're spending just doing nothing and wasting your breath on pointless conversations. Be a doer!

Going to School: The Eternal Student

As mentioned in another chapter, education is essential. I don't really know if there is any such thing as too much education, but I have witnessed many people who waste quality time going to school, because they don't have the courage to make up their mind and begin a career. They can convince themselves that they want to become an accountant until they get a degree and are ready to start working. Then, they decide that accounting isn't really for them, so they apply for law school. After law school, there just doesn't seem to be an exciting life behind chasing ambulances, so they suddenly find themselves in medical school. Before long, they are thirty-five years old and haven't worked a day or earned any serious money. Student loans are maxed out, and they're running out of degrees to earn. Be decisive about what you want to become, get your education, and work.

Movies and TV

I often wonder how much better my life would be if I didn't know what a TV was. According to Nielson Media Research, the average home has more TVs than people living in it. It is also reported that the average person watches four hours and thirty-five minutes of television each day with the average home having the TV turned on for over eight hours per day.[4] My experience tells me that most of the time spent in front of the tube is not very educational or fulfilling.

If you're watching television anywhere close to the average mentioned above, cut your cables and get a life. There are a bazillion better things that you could be doing with your time, so avoid the couch-potato syndrome that will destroy your level of productivity. I wouldn't even worry about owning a TV, and if I did happen to own one, I'd make sure to only have the basic free channels (no fifty to five hundred channel cable packages).

Please, just take my word for it. If you don't already have a television, keep it that way for as long as you can and you'll be better off. My wife and I had no channels to watch for the first year of our marriage, but when we hooked up the cable so that we could get a better deal on the Internet (it was actually cheaper to pay for both than just the Internet), I realized that we were suddenly wasting way more time staring at whatever pointless program happened to be on.

I'm a huge fan of movies and love to relax in my home movie theater, but too much of a good thing can be counter-productive. I hope I don't sound like a hypocrite in this section, because I do watch movies and I do watch TV. My wife would choke me if I tried to get rid of them, and I wouldn't really want to anyway, but I advise you to limit your time (as I do) when it comes to watching movies or TV. Once or twice a week to sit down and enjoy a good film is no sin, but making it an everyday priority is what you have to be careful about.

Complaining or Gossiping

Simply put—great people talk about ideas; average people talk about things; small people talk about other people.[5] Complaining will get you nowhere, and gossiping will get you there even faster. It is so repelling to be around those who badmouth every person, policy, and procedure they can think of. Do you want to be that pessimistic individual who carries a bad vibe everywhere he goes? Even if we only indulge every once in a while and vent for a brief moment, we should realize the results of our actions. Nothing good will come of a sour attitude, so regulate your tendency to complain and gossip.

Conclusion

Now that you have read this chapter and understand that you can't have a life if you want to be successful, let's get going! Just kidding . . . I hope you understood from what was written in each section that most of the time wasters listed above are perfectly okay to do. We just have to be careful about the amount of time we dedicate to these things.

Do all things in moderation. If you study too much, you'll miss out on other things. I had a good friend I lived with that either studied, worked, or slept. We'd see him about twice a week and barely even had the opportunity to speak. He completely sacrificed dating so that he could land a job doing computer animated cartoons. I don't judge him for that, but I know life would've been a little brighter for him with a better balance in his schedule. In the four months that I shared an apartment with him, he did not go on one single date! Overdoing some things in my opinion is just a waste of time. Prioritizing is obviously a personal matter, but knowing how to balance work, studies, dating, sleeping, and playing is necessary for making good use of your time.

Also, be decisive about what you're going to accomplish and when. Just floating through college waiting for decisions to be made for you is not the quickest way to prosperity. Be prayerful and seek inspiration in the choices you make. Knowing that Heavenly Father is on your side and wants the best for you is great motivation to follow your passions. You will find peace and joy as you keep the commandments and exercise your agency to live out your dreams in a righteous manner. This is a great stage in your life, so don't waste time in idleness. The sooner you get into your studies, dating, career, investments, and spiritual service, the more fulfilling your life will be.

There's a very obvious reason that President David O. McKay said, "Let us teach them to work, and to realize that the privilege to work is a gift, that the power to work is a blessing, that love to work is success."[6]

EXERCISE:

Take five minutes to identify at least three of the above mentioned time wasters that might be slowing you down. Write down on a note card that you can pin onto the wall above your pillow the three pitfalls you will work on. Calculate how much time you spend doing each of those three things in a typical week, and set a goal to cut that time in half. As you analyze the time you are spending or wasting on these things and strive to cut down on that time, you will see that your productivity will increase significantly. Get rid of your TV or Internet if that's what it takes, but just make sure you are spending more time focusing on the meaningful goals you have set for yourself and wasting less time on useless activities.

On the flip side of how not to be unproductive is focusing on being more productive. I recommend reading through Stephen R. Covey's book, *The Seven Habits of Highly Effective People.* As an LDS author, Covey strikes a certain cord in my life and inspires motivation. I'm sure his books will do the same for you.

Notes

1. Matt Lewis Band, "Killing Time," 2004. Used with permission.
2. M. Russell Ballard, CES Fireside, Brigham Young University, 3 March 2002.
3. Susan Young Gates, *Life Story of Brigham Young* (Freeport, New York: Books for Libraries Press, 1971), 192.
4. *USA Today,* Sept. 21, 2006.
5. Author unknown.
6. Llewelyn R. McKay, comp., *True to the Faith* (Salt Lake City: Bookcraft, 1966), 287.

16

Surround Yourself with Ambition and Success

Two months off of the mission, I found myself going to BYU—a college that I never planned on attending. I lived at a large, popular apartment complex called Liberty Square with a guy I had met down in Peru as a missionary. Lucky for me, because I didn't know anybody else who was going to BYU, he turned out to be one of the best influences a guy could hope for in this life. Over the next several years, I was fortunate enough to become friends with several inspiring individuals from ages eighteen to ninety-five. Each contributed to the force that drives me to become a better person.

One of my companions lived about an hour away from BYU campus, and he had also served with my roommate for a little while in Peru. We'd get together about once a month to reminisce about the mission and go out and try to score some phone numbers from the ladies. These were my first two afterlife buddies. Both were very money oriented and had fantastic dreams with great ideas about how to accomplish them.

Before I continue with this story that has a vital point, let me just say that BYU is a gold mine for driven, inspirational individuals who serve as great examples for somebody like me and you. It is a very competitive university to be accepted into, but if you can find a way to get in, I highly recommend going for it. Not only are you surrounded by exceptional students, but each ward is blessed with an outstanding bishopric from the surrounding communities. I'm not saying that it's the only place . . . just that I recommend it. It's not a bad scene for a returned missionary out and about looking for an eternal companion either!

Seeing the Light

I was already tackling some of the prerequisite classes to get into dental school and still trying to decide on a major. I soon started to lean towards linguistics since I enjoyed the Portuguese and French classes I was already enrolled in. That was my master plan . . . study tongues for a while and then move on to the teeth! I had never even considered doing anything else. I figured out when I was about sixteen that dentists could afford million dollar homes and set their own schedules . . . what more could you really want in a job?

After a night out with the guys, we'd usually head back to the apartment to eat some pizza and chitchat before going to sleep. The first several times we did this, my companion and my roommate would talk about these visionary plans on how they were going to earn large sums of money. It was such a foreign thought process for me that I usually just left the room with the notion that I had better ways to waste my time.

My roommate was about to enter into law school and then go work for his dad's firm, but he wanted to prove to them that he was worthy of his hire. He wanted them to beg for him to come join their team because of his amazing ability to accumulate wealth. Everything was laid out for him from the time he was a youngster. He had eight brothers, all of whom were either doctors or lawyers, and they coached him along the easiest and quickest path to joining the family law firm. They had a great family vision to establish the Church in southeast Texas and maintain a happy, comfortable life with their families. My roommate already had his spot reserved; all he really needed to do was find a wife to bring home and get through law school as soon as possible, but he felt an urgency to demonstrate that he would be an asset to the family business.

My companion was an undergraduate student with an English major at Weber State College. He had gone through high school competing in business-oriented academics. He is still the only guy I've ever met that actually understood the concept of business before he graduated from high school.

When my companion and my roommate would get together, they shared their latest discoveries that would lead to wealth. I honestly thought that they were lunatics to constantly brainstorm about their grand business schemes. The pens would come out and drawings on the greasy pizza napkins would map out the latest financial secrets that had been conceived. I already knew what I wanted to do, and I knew that the world expected me to do something along the lines of what I was on my way to doing. Getting all excited about some far-fetched, impossible venture just didn't interest me at all.

I was already enveloped in this environment of people who were wanting to do things a little out of the ordinary. Unfortunately, my eyes were still blinded by the culture that I grew up in. Lucky for me, my father sent me a care package one day with a book that soon altered my mentality in a way that I can never go back. It was a small book that was easy to read called *Rich Dad, Poor Dad* by Robert Kiyosaki. If you haven't read it, find a copy and don't put it down until you've finished.

Compare it to a seed as Alma 32 does with the parable of faith. Compare it to a small spark that becomes a blazing fire. Whatever the analogy, the bottom line is that I started learning about money and I haven't been able to stop! Just as a thousand forests can be created by one small acorn, a man's financial empire can be created with only a penny (or nothing but a will for that matter). My ambitious friends and family had opened up a new dimension of thought for me.

With this knowledge and inspiration that I received from the book my father had sent me, I began to understand the point of my roommate and my companion talking so much about money. I began to develop my own ideas that could potentially earn a profit in the near future. I then began to share my ideas with my roommate and we'd explore the possibilities of carrying out the plans. We discussed buying things that we could sell on eBay, we discussed importing goods from Peru, and we flirted with the idea of owning real estate. Within a year, I realized I didn't need to be a dentist to have the kind of life I desired. Also, spending half a day with my sister in a dentists office while she had surgery brought me to a realization—I would be bored out of my mind if dentistry were my everyday occupation . . . not to mention my super sense of smell and all of the bad breath I'd inhale day after day.

As a note, my roommate is currently an attorney who doesn't really practice law. He dedicates his time to a successful partnership where he has ownership of four medical clinics throughout the state of Texas. He is very happy and has fantastic goals to be doing bigger and better things within the next five years. My companion lives in Utah and makes a killing off of residential land development. He works from his brand new, gigantic home coming and going as he pleases with nobody to answer to but himself and his technical boss (his wife). Both of these close friends are well on there way to becoming multi-millionaires!

Those You Associate With Always Influence Your Thoughts and Actions

Being around motivated individuals pushed me in a whole new direction. Life took on a new meaning as I explored the financial philosophies of friends, family, leaders, and book authors. It is a natural, recurring process that takes place in our lives on a daily basis. We are surrounded by other people, and they rub off on us! Situating yourself among intelligent, motivated, and goal-oriented people will establish a contagious environment that can inspire great accomplishments in your future. Not actively networking with such people or surrounding yourself with average and subpar individuals will lead to stagnation or even digression.

George Washington was known for surrounding himself with the best men available. Is it any wonder how the first president of our country was so successful at laying a foundation for what would become a glorious nation? The men he chose to associate with, such as Benjamin Franklin, are also reported to have focused on socializing with other ambitious and influential people.

Seek Out People Who Aspire Higher

To be honest, not many individuals I've come across dream big. I'm not saying that going to medical school to become a doctor or finishing your MBA to work in international business isn't a real dream, but there are some people out there who have goals to do much more than the norm. They want to be a doctor *and* achieve large amounts of passive income (money that you generate without really having to put effort into it). They want to retire early so they can serve missions or dedicate their time to a greater cause. They want to be the Bill Gates who distributes over 10 billion dollars a year in charitable donations (I guess I could settle for being able to only donate around 1 billion).

Some can only see themselves working an 8:00-4:00 job for thirty-five or forty years with a nice house that's fully mortgaged, a couple of cars, a few toys, and a week or two of vacation every year. They save up funds in a 401k plan and create portfolios of low risk investments that they can retire off of when they turn sixty-five. Others would rather set their own schedule, be their own boss, live in a bigger house, have a few more toys, take more vacation time, and be able to retire when they're fifty. Heck—why not forty, when you're young enough to still have some fun? Actually, I think everybody wants this, but there are very few who believe in themselves enough to attempt it. Being around people who are willing to try is like a fountain of motivation.

Arrange Your Schedule to Spend Time with the Go-Getters

I make it a point to go out for lunch or play a round of golf with somebody that I can learn from almost every day. I love to be around people who operate their own businesses, because they're the ones who inspire me. Having lunch with a guy who plays 50 percent of the time, sleeps 30 percent of the time, and works 20 percent of the time, and whose bank account is loaded, makes me want to find ways to make it happen for me.

I love to get together with acquaintances in the real estate market who are literally making a fortune, because if they can do it, so can I if I listen closely to their strategies. I love to get nosey and ask all sorts of questions to the guy who has earned himself a handsome profit off of the stock market in the last month . . . handsome equals more money than what most people make in a year!

Success Spreads like a Wildfire

It's the same concept that helped you be a better missionary in the field. Every month or so, your mission president sent his assistants and your zone leaders out to share goals and accomplishments with you. They'd show you how many discussions a certain companionship, district, or zone had taught during a week. Eyes would light up and every missionary in the room would gawk as the number of converts who were baptized in a certain area was revealed during the reports.

Then, they'd share with you how it was done. They'd focus on key factors that influenced the success of the missionary effort. You'd leave those training meetings pumped up and excited about applying your newly formed vision. Meeting after meeting, you became a better missionary because of the example of other missionaries, and you could see the effect that it had on the fruits of your labor.

The exact same concept holds true in the world of monetary gain. The more successful and brilliant people you can surround yourself with, the more inspired, motivated, and knowledgeable you will be when it comes to creating your own abundance. Meeting after meeting, you will develop new ideas and new strategies that will make you a better businessman.

Be friends with everybody, of course, regardless of their pocket book, but make sure you buddy up with people who are doing big things in life. It is absolutely necessary to keep you on your toes and performing to the best of your ability.

Exercise:

Identify two individuals who are already successful in a way that you would like to be. Then, think of two friends who are ahead in the game at the moment and have all the right ideas to do big things in life. Make an effort to spend time with these individuals on a weekly basis and delve into financial conversations every chance you get.

17

Continue to Serve

> We frequently call the brethren to go on missions to preach the Gospel, and they will go and labor as faithfully as men can do, fervent in spirit, in prayer, in laying on hands, in preaching to and teaching the people how to be saved. In a few years they come home, and throwing off their coats and hats, they will say, 'Religion, stand aside, I am going to work now to get something for myself and my family.' This is folly in the extreme. When a man returns from a mission where he has been preaching the Gospel he ought to be just as ready to come to this pulpit to preach as if he were in England, France, Germany, or on the islands of the sea. And when he has been at home a week, a month, a year, or ten years, the spirit of preaching and the spirit of the Gospel ought to be within him like a river flowing forth to the people in good words, teachings, precepts, and examples. If this is not the case he does not fill his mission.[1]

While returning home with ambitions and dreams to conquer the world is commendable, it would serve us all to reiterate these words of Brigham Young. I hope that you understand clearly the principle of seeking God and his kingdom first and foremost in order to be blessed above measure. Do not now nor ever lose focus on the building up of the kingdom as priority number one . . . even if it appears to be at a cost of limited monetary gain. Remember that wealth means much more than a number of dollar bills representing your net worth.

> Though I possessed millions of money and property, that does not excuse me from performing the labor that it is my calling to perform,

> so far as I have strength and ability, any more than the poorest man in the community is excused. The more we are blessed with means, the more we are blessed with responsibility; the more we are blessed with wisdom and ability, the more we are placed under the necessity of using that wisdom and ability in the spread of righteousness, the subjugation of sin and misery, and the amelioration of the condition of mankind. The man that has only one talent and the man that has five talents have responsibility accordingly [see Matthew 25:14–30]. If we have a world of means, we have a world of responsibility.[2]

Living with the Holy Ghost as your Companion

What you learned on your mission should remain engraved upon your heart for the rest of your life. You figured out before you ever even escaped the MTC that without the Spirit, you can do nothing. Absolutely nothing! You could knock doors all day, approach every family you saw, or stand on the tallest soap box and preach with the most booming voice the gospel of salvation . . . but, if you lacked the companionship of the Holy Ghost for one reason or another, failure was the only result you'd see that day.

So how did you invite the Spirit into your missionary experience? By serving, of course! You forgot yourself and served God and your fellow man all day, every day. Your daily planners were filled to the brim with nothing but pure and holy service. This, along with total obedience and several other factors, invited the Holy Ghost into your life, and thus you emanated its influence so all of those with whom you came into contact could feel its power.

This was the number one factor that determined your success as a missionary, and it will be the number one factor that determines your success as a working husband and father. Parley P. Pratt proclaimed that the Holy Ghost assists a man in becoming like God. He said,

> The gift of the Holy Spirit . . . quickens all the intellectual faculties, increases, enlarges, expands and purifies all the natural passions and affections; and adapts them, by the gift of wisdom, to their lawful use. It inspires, develops, cultivates and matures all the fine-toned sympathies, joys, tastes, kindred feelings and affections of our nature. It inspires virtue, kindness, goodness, tenderness, gentleness and charity. It develops beauty of person, form and features. It tends to health, vigor, animation and social feeling. It develops and invigorates all the

> faculties of the physical and intellectual man. It strengthens, invigorates, and gives tone to the nerves. In short, it is, as it were, marrow to the bone, joy to the heart, light to the eyes, music to the ears, and life to the whole being.[3]

Pratt goes on to explain how we are drawn to those individuals who possess the Holy Ghost. It is attractive!

At the root of almost every business transaction is a relationship, and due to the fact that people will be drawn to you because of the kind of person you are, opportunity will abound in your life. You will see door after door open up and give you ultimate control over your financial situation. Make sure you are worthy of the Holy Ghost and things will work out for you. Invite the Holy Ghost by serving God and serving your fellow man.

Once a Missionary, Always a Missionary!

Serving a mission was one of the most honorable privileges that you will ever be blessed with. "After all that has been said, the greatest and most important duty is to preach the gospel" said Joseph Smith.[4] By continuing to open your mouth and share the gospel as with the voice of an angel, you will merit prosperity in this life. Opportunity to serve others both spiritually and temporally will surely abound. Take advantage of it. There is no concept more simple or glorious: obey God's commandments, and he will bless you.

Some call it sacrifice, but I don't believe that giving something small in exchange for something great quite qualifies as the definition of sacrifice. In my mind, the semantics just don't fit. I have never met one individual who served for the right reasons who didn't feel like he got so much more out of his mission than what he put into it. By giving of yourself for the rest of your life as you did in the mission field, you will see the windows of heaven open and blessings pour down upon you and your family.

Continue to do missionary work when the name tag is no longer worn and the white shirt and ties are hanging in the closet. Just because you've tossed the old, worn-out shoes and framed your name tag doesn't mean you're not a missionary anymore. "Once a missionary, always a missionary" is what my mission president would preach from the pulpit at zone conferences. Seek out opportunities to share the message of the Restoration, and most certainly do not shy away from an opportunity presented.

The chance to share your testimony comes far less often when you return home, so don't let one single moment of truth pass you by. It invites the Spirit, and you feel it more powerfully and distinctly than ever.

As a missionary, you feel the influence of the Holy Ghost all day every day because you're out teaching lessons . . . that's why a mission is such a happy time in your life. When going to college, dating, and doing what you need to do to pay the bills, the environment just isn't quite the same as when you're teaching people to pray and communicate with God for the very first time in their lives or explaining to them the path to eternal happiness.

What I'm saying is that, you don't feel the Spirit as often or as strongly as you did when you were out in the field. For this reason, you really notice it when you seize an opportunity to share the truth with somebody after your mission. The Holy Ghost helps you to say the right words, and you know that he will feel the power behind your testimony. By continuing your efforts to bring the gospel and its saving ordinances into the lives of those you meet, you are serving God and serving man. In return, you are blessed with a greater portion of the Spirit that will help you achieve success in your endeavors.

One of your greatest challenges will be complacency in the gospel. Yes, you might go through the motions by reading your scriptures and praying daily, but all too often, a returned missionary can lose his spiritual drive. I am convinced that the number one way to feed fuel to the fire is by bearing testimony of the restored gospel. I don't mean just sitting around and waiting for somebody to ask for an explanation about the Church. I'm saying be forward and open about your convictions by searching out opportunities to share what you know.

Temple Service

Another way you should continue to serve is by attending the temple and doing your family history work. As a missionary, you were dedicated to serving the living. Many missionaries go a whole two years without going through or even seeing a temple. It is such a privilege to go there and perform ordinances vicariously once you return home. President Gordon B. Hinckley spoke of a woman who performed the temple ordinances for over 20,000 people before she passed away. He spoke of the large reception that would welcome her into the spirit world with gratitude and joy for the *service* she rendered.[5] What a phenomenal accomplishment and example she left for us. You can participate in the redeeming of the dead as often as you make time to, and I highly recommend frequent visits to the temple to do so.

Go Outside Your Bubble in Your New Wards

Be active and outgoing in your new wards and *grow where you are planted.* Go out of your way to meet everybody and become friends with the members who surround you. You will be tempted to believe that they should fellowship you since you are new, but unless you end up in a perfect little piece of Zion, you will have to go outside of your comfort zone and make the first move in becoming acquainted. Not knowing everybody in your ward will certainly limit your opportunity to participate.

Once you get past the new-kid-on-the-block stage, it's easy to serve in your ward. People might be moving in or out of their homes, so there's always room for a helping hand. Older families often times need help in the yard or with groceries. The families you are assigned to home teach need your friendship and priesthood authority. Create opportunities that involve getting to know all of the faces in your ward. It's worth the effort.

Service Your Ward while Prioritizing Church and Work

Your good example and unique personality can be such an asset to the ward in which you reside, and you will find that the Lord has prepared special callings for you to hold while living there. It doesn't matter if you are called to be the Elders' quorum president, a nursery teacher, or a counselor in the bishopric . . . each is a capacity that will help you learn and grow. Just because one calling doesn't seem as important as another is no reason not to serve and magnify your duties 110 percent. Make time to fulfill your calling, and you will see that there will be time enough for everything else.

One dangerous habit to avoid would be dedicating too much time to your work and not enough time to prayer, scripture study, church callings, Sunday meetings, family activities, and temple attendance. Do not fool yourself into thinking that you're the exception to the rule and that God understands your situation. Satan tries to instill this mindset into the working man's soul. He would have you believe that you are being a Saint by choosing to take the Sunday shift at work, because "somebody has to do it and it might as well be a person who is already spiritually strong."

Use Your Wealth Wisely

The brilliant tempter would deceive you into believing that God is dependent upon you and your income. How many times have you heard a man proclaim his righteous desires to be rich so that he can pay a large sum of tithing? Pure garbage! God never has been and never will be dependent on a man for his tithing, and a man who believes the contrary is arrogant. The Lord can have money as He pleases with or without the help of a man who is nothing.

You can, however, do very righteous things with the money that you are blessed with. In fact, if you opt not to, use them wisely there's a good possibility that you could lose the privilege of riches. There are several ways to apply your earnings towards acts of service. Some donate extra money to the church missionary fund in order to help send those of less fortunate economies or circumstances on a mission. Some buy wheelchairs for the handicapped children of Honduras. Many make it a point to help out the hungry, naked, and homeless *every* chance they get. A select few provide a private jet for the leaders of the church! The options are endless and always present.

I've heard rumors of a wealthy member of the Church who was asked if he paid a full 10 percent for tithing, and he responded that he only kept 10 percent for himself and donated the rest. It's no coincidence that a man with such a giving heart has been blessed with much to give. Others of great riches have been known to donate as much as one third of their entire net worth to those in need. By channeling your prosperity into a means of serving others, you are proving yourself worthy of such wealth. Please, do not misunderstand—service should be rendered out of the goodness of your heart and not with the intentions of self-gain.

The Only Way Up Is By Lifting Others Up Along the Way

Money or not, there will be daily opportunities to serve. Pray that you will receive these opportunities to exhibit the Christlike attributes of love, charity, compassion, and humility. If for some reason, you don't feel like there are occasions to serve, be proactive about the situation and create them. One way or another, you must focus on the welfare of those around you in order to accomplish greatness. An essential principle of progression that I've heard about is no man can prosper without making sure that his fellow man is prospering at the same time.

Serve Those You Served in Your Mission

Lastly, continue to serve those members and converts whom you were privileged to meet in your mission. I wish I could put into words the happiness that I've felt after my mission as I've stayed in contact with converts, members, and companions.

I've learned of several individuals I had the privilege of baptizing whom have served or are serving missions themselves. I've seen families sealed in the temple. I've seen members on the verge of falling away who are now steadfast in the gospel. I've seen companions who now have beautiful families and happy lives. As a matter of fact, I spoke with three of my companions on the phone recently . . . with no intentions of writing about it. It's just a part of my life now to stay in touch with those I grew to love. By following president Hinckley's counsel to write your converts, you are continuing to fulfill that sacred calling you were given.

Blessings through Service

Understand that serving others is an essential step in building your own wealth. Service is one of life's catalysts that speeds up our rate of progression. It is an eternal principle that you are fully entitled to apply and experiment upon during your mortal journey. Blessings are promised to you and your family if you maintain the spirit of service in your daily life. That doesn't necessarily mean that you will be rewarded monetarily for your righteousness, but you will be blessed in one form or another.

Remember what you learned from the whole-hearted act of serving a mission, and maintain that disposition throughout your marriage and career. Continue to serve God first and foremost with all your might, mind, and strength. The blessings will vary and are not always immediate, which is why some don't recognize the benefits of serving. Those with faith and the proper attitude in serving others will certainly be rewarded both temporally and eternally.

Exercises:

In your prayers tonight and from here on out, ask for the opportunity to serve. I promise you that you will recognize an abundance of these opportunities. Remember that being able to serve will not always work out to the convenience of your schedule, but make small sacrifices to demonstrate that you are willing to put others before yourself.

Also, go to the temple this week. You know you have time, so make it happen.

Lastly, be a 100 percent home teacher every month for the rest of your life. It is a small and simple responsibility that truly reveals your desires to fulfill your gospel duties.

Notes

1. Brigham Young, *Discourses of Brigham Young,* sel. John A. Widtsoe (Salt Lake City: Deseret Book, 1954), 328–29.
2. Ibid., 315.
3. Parley P. Pratt, *Key to the Science of Theology,* 61–62.
4. Joseph Smith, *The Teachings of the Prophet Joseph Smith,* sel. Joseph Fielding Smith (Salt Lake City: Deseret Book, 1976), 113.
5. Gordon B. Hinckley, "The Things of Which I Know" *Ensign*, May 2007, 83–85.

18

CONCLUSION

Herein, I've mentioned several other books and suggested you read them. This book was written as a general guide to open your eyes and lead you in the right direction towards financial knowledge that will assist you in your life. Many of the chapters only skim the surface of subjects that have volumes of literature written about them with much greater detail than what I have written. I do not claim to be an expert in any particular field. I am certain, however, that the information shared in these pages will enable you to graduate from college debt free, own some significant investments, and have money reserves in your bank account. Please consider my invitation to continue your quest for knowledge that will give you an advantage in the world of finances. Learning to prosper is the first step

I hope you noticed that I repeatedly used the verb *do* in my writings. It really is as simple as that. Either you *do* the things that lead to wealth, or you just read about them and say to yourself, "Gee, that's interesting stuff. I'm sure I'll want to apply it one day." If you can't *do* the exercises I suggest in each chapter, I can honestly say that you won't benefit at all from this lecture. Forget the excuses, forget the procrastination, and *do* something extraordinary with your life.

Your mission is something you have to cherish for the rest of your life. It is a part of who you are, and may it always be a source of inspiration as you decide on the quality of person you wish to become and the quality of life you wish to have. Honor your divine experience by holding true to the principles that you incorporated into your life as a servant of the Lord.

Missionary habits invite the Spirit, and the influence of the Spirit will be the most essential ingredient in your quest for prosperity.

Life is good! The opportunities that abound with financial prosperity will enable you to bring so much *more* good into the world. Rich or poor, we must always put Heavenly Father first in our lives and willingly demonstrate our love for Him. We must strive to keep our priorities straight and never let the love of money come between us and our exaltation. Please evaluate your spiritual progression often and beware of pride. If you ever notice digression in your relationship with God, do whatever it takes to remedy the situation and get back on track. An obsession with riches can destroy relationships—with the Lord and with your family.

Work hard and do your best to be successful in every aspect of life as it relates to the gospel in its entirety. The happiness and satisfaction you find as you balance work, play, and rest will fill your heart with gratitude and a desire to do good works. As you continue to build the kingdom, you will be blessed beyond measure.

About the Author

Dustin Robison was born in 1981 and raised in southeast Texas. He served a mission in Lima, Peru, and afterwards graduated from BYU with a bachelor's degree in linguistics and a bachelor's degree in Portuguese. There, he met and married the love of his life, Caren Deppe. He taught Spanish at the MTC for three years before becoming a successful entrepreneur and investor.

0 26575 52323 2